Jimmy Hoffa is Missing
The Gap
July 30, 1975
(2:30-3:30 pm)

By David W. Tubman

Enjoy the read, ANDREA !!

David W. Tubman

Published by JHIM-The Gap LLC   New Braunfels, Texas

A Long-Held Family Secret-Until Now!

Paperback-ISBN #978-1-64970-706-2

HOW TO PURCHASE BOOKS:

Give Me Money-I give you book.

Printed in the United States of America

First Edition: July-2020

Hoffa Family July 19th, 1957
James P, Barbara Ann, James R & Josephine

Dedicated to the Hoffa family

I pray for the Hoffa family for all the years they have suffered
from the absence of their father, husband, grandfather.
And for a continued break from the evil of the past,
which swallowed up lives and livelihoods.
May God continue to create great distance
from the heartaches and many unfulfilled dreams.

There is no such thing as "Closure" when a loved one has passed.
May we all realize that life is God-given
and that everyone is precious in His sight - DWTubman

DISCLAIMER DECLARATION

The author and publisher declare that <u>by no means</u> does the
book constitute any charges of guilt nor innocence
of anyone named in its content.
Therefore, all persons mentioned are presumed to be innocent
unless they have been formally charged and
prosecuted in a court of law.
All information presented herein was formerly provided to
FBI authorities, or was already freely available
in the public domain.
I, the author, was not a direct eyewitness to the actual events
that took place on July 30, 1975.
However, I did hear the accounts directly from the
eyewitnesses within 24-36 hours of the events they had witnessed.
Many of the details of their story were not mentioned by news
agencies until much later. Still, other significant information has
never been made public. Some of those details are about to be
discussed. Although I do personally consider their testimony as
100% factual, all combined evidence presented is still
circumstantial, yet extraordinarily convincing.
Review the details inside and then form your own conclusions.
To the FBI and other law enforcement,
-You had your chance and missed it.

Author: David W. Tubman and Publisher: JHIM-The Gap LLC

Jimmy Hoffa is Missing
The Gap

CONTENTS

Introduction

"Jimmy Hoffa Is Missing"

This was the main headline that appeared on the front page of The Detroit Free Press-Metro Edition on August 1, 1975. It was the first announcement of the disappearance of James Riddle Hoffa two days after he vanished from The Machus Red Fox Restaurant in Bloomfield Township, Michigan. Jimmy Hoffa was President of the Teamsters Union in Detroit from 1957 to 1971. Everyone knew who he was. A large percentage of Detroit's workers were likely members of the labor unions, and Jimmy Hoffa was the man in charge, so this was stunning news.

'The Gap' (2:30-3:30 pm)

This was the 60-Minute Gap in time that Chuckie O'Brien's alibi could never seem to fill. The FBI was inundated with hundreds, if not thousands of leads and sightings of Jimmy Hoffa. The witnesses were few, and they narrowed the suspects down to a single individual, Charles Lenton 'Chuckie' O'Brien. What he had to say to the FBI when they interviewed him on two occasions was all-important in trying to understand the events surrounding Hoffa that Wednesday afternoon on July 30, 1975.

But his alibis were scattered and difficult to pin down. They zeroed in on a 60-minute time period, which I call 'The Gap.' Where was Chuckie O'Brien from 2:30 to 3:30 pm? That would be the major thrust of their ensuing investigation that would never be resolved.

"Last Seen Outside Restaurant"

This was the tag line printed above the main headline. Several people identified Jimmy Hoffa at the Machus Red Fox restaurant during the 2:00-2:45 pm time frame. Two men shook Hoffa's hand; another saw him making phone calls at a nearby pay-phone outside of Dammon Hardware. Others recognized Jimmy Hoffa as he sat just behind the driver in the maroon-colored Mercury. Three other men were in the car with him as the Mercury was idling in the side driveway, getting ready to leave.

The last known sighting of Jimmy Hoffa was around 2:30 pm by the driver of a delivery truck who was entering the same driveway as the Mercury was pulling out. He saw it turn right onto Telegraph Road and head south. Nobody else has come forward to offer any fresh evidence about what happened next. Where did the Mercury go from there with Jimmy Hoffa seated in the back seat? Since 1975 the question has remained unanswered.

That is-Until Now!

The Cover Photos:

The two photos I chose for the cover are of a maroon 1975 Mercury Marquis Brougham sedan. This is not the actual vehicle but is identical to the model car that Joey Giacalone loaned to Chuckie O'Brien. O'Brien admits that he drove the car all day long. He admits he even drove in the 'vicinity' of The Red Fox at about the same time Hoffa went missing at 2:30 pm. But insisted Jimmy Hoffa was not in the car with him.

The photograph of the rear seat depicts where Jimmy Hoffa was last seen alive as he sat in the back of the 1975 Mercury Marquis Brougham. It was going from The Red Fox to a destination unknown. "Last Seen Outside Restaurant" would be a statement repeated for the next forty-five years.

Where's Jimmy Hoffa?

The eyewitness statements within these pages will account for and answer that very question. This book will enhance what was known with additional facts from direct eyewitnesses that observed the Mercury as it was leaving the Red Fox. They would drive side by side with the car for the next several miles and watched as it arrived at its next stop.

Jimmy Hoffa is Missing
The Gap
July 30, 1975
(2:30-3:30 pm)

By David W. Tubman

CHAPTER 1
Prologue
The Long-Held Family Secret

The story I am about to reveal within these pages was not told to the police back in 1975 when it happened. But for a good reason. I will explain that part of the story. But to be fair to the eyewitnesses, you might hold back on the condemning question that automatically comes to the tip of the tongue: "Why didn't they go to the police?" I might pose that same question to the reader. The events my parents, Kenneth and Frances Tubman saw, took them by surprise. It was a warm summer Wednesday afternoon as they were on the way to their daughter's house to enjoy a family camp out for two nights together.

They lived in the same town as the Machus Red Fox, which was Bloomfield Township, Michigan. Their usual route of travel was from their rented townhome, which was on Woodward Avenue just north of 15-mile/Maple Road. They would travel down Woodward to Maple, turn right and once they reached Telegraph Road, turn left and continue south on Hwy. 24 to Michigan Avenue. From there, it was one more right turn and a short distance over to Westland, where my sister lived. It is about a 1-hour 20-minute drive on a Wednesday with light traffic.

I will provide many details in the upcoming chapters, but I'll summarize to set the stage. To those familiar with the abduction of Jimmy Hoffa, you already know that at the intersection of Maple and Telegraph was a high-end restaurant called "The Machus Red Fox." The reason Jimmy Hoffa was there on July 30, 1975, was because he was eager to regain the head of the Teamsters union. He needed the support of arch-rival Tony Provenzano to clear the way for him to run. Hoffa was to meet with Tony Provenzano, from New Jersey, Tony Giacalone from Detroit, and Leonard Schultz, who owned the Southfield Athletic Club in Southfield. Apparently, Schultz was integral to the discussions about to take place with Hoffa at 2:00 pm that afternoon.

The Red Fox was only a place to rendezvous, not the actual meeting place, as Jimmy Hoffa did not dress in a coat and tie, which was the Red Fox dress code required to be seated inside. Hoffa arrived at 2:00, right on time, but the others were late. Actually, they didn't show up at all. Provenzano was seen as he was playing cards in the union hall in New Jersey at the same time as the scheduled meeting. Meanwhile, Tony Giacalone was busy checking his watch for the correct time with people all day long at the Southfield Athletic Club (Leonard Schultz's business).

James Riddle Hoffa had a 'Type-A' personality, personified. Promptness was a requirement of his, so when the others didn't appear for the meeting, it incensed him. He paced the parking lot then went inside The Red Fox looking for his meeting partners and spoke to a waitress and the hostess. Then he went outside again and scanned the parking lot. He walked a short distance behind the restaurant to Dammon Hardware, where there was a pay phone mounted on one of the posts, and made two phone calls. The first was to his wife, Josephine, at 2:15 pm (confirmed). He was upset about the no shows and told her he was going to come home and cook the steaks, as he had promised before leaving home earlier.

Then he immediately made a second call to Louis Linteau at Airport Service Lines. Two men, one a Real Estate agent, introduced themselves and shook Hoffa's hand when they recognized him. Hoffa chatted with them briefly. In the course of the conversation, Hoffa made mention about his wife, Josephine, and about her upcoming cataract surgery. A topic that was not public knowledge, and only Jimmy Hoffa himself could have described to them.

It was about 2:30 pm when the maroon Mercury Marquis had arrived and was spotted as it idled in the driveway on the southeast corner of the strip center, next to the Red Fox. Hoffa was seen getting into the vehicle where three other men were already seated. Witnesses said there were two men in the front and Hoffa and another man in the rear seat, directly behind the driver.

The Mercury idled briefly, then as the maroon car began to leave, a delivery truck was entering by the same driveway. The Mercury had veered towards him and forced him to hit the brakes as it almost collided with the delivery truck. The car then turned right and headed south onto Telegraph Road, never to be seen again.

Thus, the newspaper tag line, "Last Seen Outside Restaurant." If it weren't for the gruesome fate of Jimmy Hoffa that day, it's like the Mercury just rode off into the sunset, like the ending to a novel. That's where the statement has remained and has baffled the authorities and investigators for the past forty-five years. The main focal point of the investigation has always been centered around when Hoffa first arrived at the Machus Red Fox, and when people saw him last.

'The Gap' is the critical 60-minute time period when Jimmy Hoffa was abducted from the Red Fox that Wednesday, July 30, 1975, and where he was taken afterward. The 1-hour period between 2:30 and 3:30 pm needed answers that nobody was able or willing to give them.

What if I could convince you there is more information, and that's not all there is?

Nobody has since come forward with any additional information about where the Mercury went to next. The authorities had suspects and witnesses but were never able to piece together the bits and pieces of information gathered from them. So, the last known clue was the moment when the 1975 Mercury departed from the Red Fox. The car veers out of the driveway. All of the witnesses agreed that the time was 2:30 pm when they saw Jimmy Hoffa seated in the back as it exited the driveway and turned right onto Telegraph (Hwy-24).

Telegraph Road was the most traveled route connecting Detroit to the Northwest suburbs around Southfield, Pontiac, and many of the small lakes up in that area. There are a couple of freeways that crisscross Hwy-24 within a few short miles as you head south from The Red Fox at 15-Mile and Telegraph. The FBI had way too many possibilities to consider when trying to pick up the trail from that point on. Unfortunately, "Last seen outside restaurant" only pointed them to southbound Telegraph Road, and that's all they knew for sure. The top street map image shows the side driveway of the Red Fox Restaurant. It forces vehicles to only make a right turn onto Telegraph. There is a grassy center divider between the four lanes heading in each direction, with turnouts and traffic signals spread along the roadway leading toward Detroit from Maple Road in Bloomfield Township.

Google Street View © 2020 Google. Telegraph Road Heading South

1975 Maroon Mercury Marquis Brougham Sedan   Jimmy Hoffa seen in Rear Seat

© 2020 Copyright-DWTubman/Mercury-Back Seat Image

Where's JIMMY HOFFA
Call (313)962-

James P. Hoffa Prints Bumper Stickers/Offered $200,000 REWARD

© 2020 Copyright-DWTubman/Remastered Bumper Sticker

The maroon-colored Mercury in the photograph represents a very distinct type of vehicle. It was unmistakably described by the many witnesses that day. The spacious rear seat image shows that there is enough room for two big men on the seat with plenty of room on the floor. I contend that the floor area was occupied by Jimmy Hoffa immediately after the vehicle departed.

The 'Long-held family secret' begins as the Mercury veers out from the Red Fox.

My mother and father (Ken and Frances) were invited to join my sister and her family for a 2-night campout at Pinkney Lake from Wednesday, July 30 to Friday, August 1, 1975. I was living with my parents at the time to conserve money for my upcoming move to the West Coast in early 1976. They rented a 2-story townhome in Bloomfield Township at Bloomfield Terrace on Woodward Avenue. I didn't join the family for the camping trip that day, so I was not with them in the car. I'll summarize for brevity and provide full details later on. As I mentioned, the usual route took them right by The Machus Red Fox. They left their home close to 2:15 pm, and that put them at the intersection of Telegraph and 15-Mile roads at the precise moment the Mercury 'veered' out from the driveway of the Red Fox Restaurant. Note that 2:15 was the time of Jimmy Hoffa's call to Josephine. That would mean the Tubmans left home during the call to his wife.

The Tubman car was in the far-left lane going southbound on Telegraph Road (Hwy-24), passing the Red Fox Restaurant. The Mercury's erratic movement, veering out of the driveway, catches the eye of Frances, who sat in the passenger seat as Ken drove their car. Frances described it as a big maroon luxury car like a Continental. She didn't know car models, so anything big and boxy would look like a

"Lincoln" to her. She learned the model later. Incidentally, it turns out that year model Mercury and Lincoln were almost identical in body style and shape.

The Mercury pulled up tightly behind the Tubman's car and followed for a few moments. Then it pulled up right alongside in the next lane, and the two vehicles drove just a few feet apart and even with each other at the same rate of speed for the next several minutes. Frances and the driver of the Mercury exchanged stares, and then Frances notices a lot of commotion in the rear seat. Two big men were busy, violently struggling with something beneath their feet. Their knees were pushed high into their chests. Ken recognizes the driver and tells Frances, "Quit looking at them, Frances! That's the Mafia." She describes to him why she was looking so intently and what she is seeing going on in the other car, but Ken is emphatic and tells her, "Turn around! Do you want to end up in the Detroit River?"

The Mercury fell back briefly, then came up side by side a second time. It was a replay from moments before. The driver of the Mercury and my mother are having a full-blown staring contest, and the two men are still frantically fighting with something on the floorboard. I think once Ken mentioned, "That's the mafia," it made mom look even closer. She had no idea who the driver was at that time, but once she knew he was part of the Mafia, her curiosity took over. Then she had several minutes to study him carefully. My father knew who the driver was already, he was a well-known mob figure in Detroit and a likely visitor to Darby's restaurant.

The two cars continued on another mile or so until Ken started to feel uneasy. He wondered why this guy was so interested in them, and mom was making him feel all the more anxious. So, he slowed down and let the Mercury go up ahead a bit, to create some distance between them. The Mercury then sped ahead of them and turned into a well-known restaurant up ahead. Ken knew the restaurant intimately as he had been a restaurant manager in the Detroit area since we moved there in 1960. The Mercury turned into the very place dad was hired to manage during the year before in 1974. However, when he discovered it was owned by the mob the day before he was to start working there, he turned the job down. He took early retirement and didn't work again after that.

Ken and Frances slowed down enough to see the Mercury come to a complete stop behind the other restaurant. It parked behind the right rear corner of the building, with about 2/3 of the car length exposed beyond the building. So, the car was recognizable to the Tubmans as being the same car that followed them. There were other significant things observed by the Tubmans. When you read about it, you will have a clearer vision of the fate of Jimmy Hoffa. They did not see Jimmy Hoffa in the vehicle. But judging from the activity and violent movements of the men in the rear seat, they were fiercely struggling to keep something or someone from getting up from the floor.

My parents did not fully comprehend what they had seen. They felt uneasy, but they did not connect whatever was on the floorboard of the car with anything that made them feel threatened or in danger of any sort. So, they continued on their way to my sister's house. They chatted about it the rest of the way to my sister's house and a little when they got there. But they just couldn't fill in the blanks or figure out the reasons for it. The family camped on Wednesday and Thursday then headed back home on Friday, August 1, 1975.

Before we get into all the other details, I want the reader to do
something, so the story comes via the same perspective as the
eyewitnesses, Ken and Frances. First, I want you to shelve all the
conclusions you have already formed regarding what happened next. There
have been books, movies, blogs, and folklore over the last 45-years.
Everyone is bound to already have some form of foregone conclusion
about the fate of Jimmy Hoffa they have settled on.

Secondly, you must decide from the start that you will believe what
the Tubmans have to tell you. Don't worry. Once you have completed the
book, you can dust off the old foregone conclusions and start back up right
where you left off. However, I am sure you will see things quite differently
by the end of this book.

A bonus to the book is a home-video I had the foresight to create back
in 2009 before my mother, Frances, passed away in 2011. After you've
read about the testimony, you will have the unique opportunity to see her
and hear her retell it in her very own words. She was 92 years old at that
time, but as you will see, she vividly recalled the things she and my father
observed in 1975. The link is provided in Chapter 6. Please hold off
viewing it until you arrive there in the book.

I purposefully arranged the events, so the information is delivered in
the same sequence as when it was revealed to Ken and Frances and myself.
The intentional sequencing develops your viewpoint in the same way as
our perspective was formed. You have learned more about the Tubmans as
you progress through the book. By the time you arrive at the home-video
on page 51, you will be able to fully sense Frances' sincerity and genuine
nature. Then, you are also able to determine if she did an excellent job of
recalling the details accurately with the home-video.

I am in the unique position of being the son of two eyewitnesses, and
I was present at the moment Ken and Frances heard the news when it was
initially broadcast. I watched their eyes and saw the fear in their faces. I

heard it in their voices as they spoke when telling me everything they saw. It proved that what they were telling me was authentic. You have my word. It was beyond their character to make any part of it up. These are the two witnesses the FBI had only hoped for but didn't know they existed. Perhaps it would have made a difference. Perhaps not.

The Hoffa family still doesn't have the answers to what really happened to their father.

I have dedicated the book to the Hoffa family. I don't believe we ever have 'closure' when someone close to us dies. Sometimes it matters how they died, but the memories live on. But when the death is at the hands of another, we must find justice. If nobody becomes accountable, then all we have left are the answers and reasons to settle on. These new facts I present will not quell the emptiness, but offer just a few solutions to open questions. Hopefully, those few questions will be put to rest.

I best introduce the two eyewitnesses, so you may see everything through their eyes. Ken and Frances were terrific parents. Everyone knew them as very kind-hearted and caring individuals. Frances was a Virginia girl, and Ken was from Boston, making him a 'Yankee.' Somewhat different from James R. Hoffa, who was a mid-westerner from the industrial north. However, there were similarities between my father and Hoffa. Since Jimmy was born in Brazil, Indiana, on Feb 14, 1913, he and my dad were only eight months apart. Ken was born on Jun 13, 1912, in Boston, Massachusetts.

Both men earned the right to carry the label 'The Greatest Generation.' Just consider what their families endured while growing up at the beginning of the twentieth century. There was the Spanish Flu epidemic of 1918, the Roaring 20s, World War I, and 'The Great Depression' of the 30s, another World War in the 40s. It is no wonder that the men and women of that generation would be strong. They were quite capable of enduring most anything that came their way, survivalists of their time.

The life paths of Jimmy Hoffa and my father, Ken Tubman, would cross over on at least a few occasions in their lives. Perhaps it was merely coincidental. I believe it was that Ken Tubman came to know a lot about Jimmy Hoffa, but I doubt whether Mr. Hoffa ever knew who Ken Tubman was. They would never become friends and were not in the same social circles. They may have never even had a conversation between them. Yet, during their lifetimes, I can mention three times they both were in the same place at the same time.

-The first-time paths crossed was in 1957.

-The next would be in the 1960s and 70s, in Detroit.

-The final crossing was when Jimmy Hoffa and Ken Tubman would be within feet of each other. That was on that fateful afternoon of Jul 30, 1975. Jimmy Hoffa and my father were both in Miami Beach, Florida, in the year 1957. Jimmy Hoffa was about to become president of the Teamsters for the first time, and he gave his campaign acceptance speech during the convention at one of the Miami Beach hotels. My father, Ken, worked in one hotel nearby, as his passion for life was the hotel and restaurant business. During the time of the convention, he was the general manager of the Balmoral Hotel in Miami. All the big hotels were clustered up and down the Sunset Strip in Miami Beach. With a busy Teamsters convention in town, every hotel on the strip would bustle with convention-goers. That included hordes of news reporters. Jimmy Hoffa was big-time news for two reasons: He was about to succeed Dave Beck as union president, and criminal charges were being leveled by Robert Kennedy. Members of the McLellan commission were hounding Hoffa and the union. Although they were aggressively going after organized crime, Jimmy Hoffa was the primary character. Charges were pending, but he was later acquitted of those charges. This was undoubtedly when my dad would have first learned who Jimmy Hoffa was. Who knows, they may have even been in the same dining room together during the convention. Their paths were likely to have crossed in Miami, Florida, in 1957. The unions were very prevalent in Miami, and it always pitted 'the employee' against 'the management.' Ken was part of the management. Miami Beach remained one of the busiest convention towns in the 1950s. Jobs were abundant, so the situation seemed perfect for my dad.

However, in February 1959, Fidel Castro became the new President of Cuba through a revolutionary takeover. As he took the helm, he booted the Mob off the island. They were not only referred to as 'The Mafia,' but 'LCN' or 'La Cosa Nostra,' the 'Mob' or just 'organized crime.' The Mob had moved some of their criminal activities over to Havana. It was only 90 miles away, so they set up shop over in Cuba to ease the pressure they were getting in the US. Unfortunately, their presence would be short-lived. Once Castro took control, he purged the island of the societal miscreants, which he felt were poisoning the Cuban society. He expelled large segments of the population, which included the Mafia. That didn't sit well with the Mob. They would stand to lose tens of millions from the expulsion from Havana and Cuba.

Meanwhile, the US Government was desperate to figure out how to remove Castro as a bad actor so close to Florida. Well, it's been said that "The enemy of my enemy is my friend." Both the CIA and the Mob hated to have Castro in charge in Cuba and secretly tried to make joint plans for his assassination. But the individuals who the Mafia had selected for the hit eventually chickened out, and it failed miserably. Castro was sending former prisoners, patients from the mental hospitals (called 'institutions' back then), and others over to Miami. Many others fled in boats all on their own to Miami Beach in search of US amnesty. That influx of jobless people soaked up all the hospitality jobs in the area. That made wages competitive, and the salaries sunk so low that even the hospitality managers had a hard time demanding adequate wages to live on. My father was no exception, and we eventually left Miami and moved up to 'The Motor City,' where jobs and the economy were humming because of the growing automotive industry. Now we are right in Jimmy Hoffa's back yard. 'The Automotive Capital of the World.' It took years to learn how to blend in with the industrial Midwest. That was true for all of us.

Hoffa Plays Dice With A Group of Men June 11, 1957

Walter P. Reuther Library, Archives of Labor and Urban Affairs, Wayne State University

Hoffa Walks Picket Line Against Cab Co. September 30, 1948

Walter P. Reuther Library, Archives of Labor and Urban Affairs, Wayne State University

"I may have my faults, but being wrong ain't one of them."
-Jimmy Hoffa

1950s #1

Wonderful things happen at the Balmoral

1957-Hoffa gives acceptance speech at Teamsters Convention at nearby hotel in Miami Beach. The hotels were busy catering to the crowds that swarmed the city during the convention and the news crews following Hoffa.

Kenneth E. Tubman
Manager-Balmoral Hotel
Miami Beach, Florida
1956-1958

#2 1960s

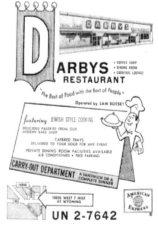

DARBYS RESTAURANT
- COFFEE SHOP
- DINING ROOM
- COCKTAIL LOUNGE

"the Best of Food with the Best of People"

Operated by SAM BOESKY

featuring JEWISH STYLE COOKING

DELICIOUS PASERIES FROM OUR MODERN BAKE SHOP

CATERED TRAYS DELIVERED TO YOUR DOOR FOR ANY EVENT

PRIVATE DINING ROOM FACILITIES AVAILABLE
AIR CONDITIONED • FREE PARKING

CARRY-OUT DEPARTMENT A SANDWICH OR A COMPLETE DINNER

10000 WEST 7 MILE AT WYOMING

AMERICAN EXPRESS

UN 2-7642

Sam Boesky-Owner-
Had ties to Purple Gang.

1960 to 1968 DARBY'S Restaurant-Detroit
Ken Tubman was General Manager (8 years) and would have greeted and escorted Hoffa and associates whenever they came to dine.

Tubman's car was once rigged to blow up during his tenure-but the incident was never reported. An apparent Mafia hit.

1970s #3

Last Fateful Crossed Path
July 30,1975

CROSSED PATHS-But Never Friends

"There is no fear in love, but perfect love casts out fear

because fear hath torment.

He that fears is not made perfect in love."

(1 John 4:18 KJV)

https://teamster.org/content/teamster-history-visual-timeline

Chapter 2
Detroit, Michigan
The Mafia & The Restaurant Business

The paths of Jimmy Hoffa and my father, Ken Tubman, crossed again during the 1960s.

That was a period when fear and intimidation ran amok in Detroit. The mafia exploited their reputation of violence, and that enabled organized crime to keep its foothold in Detroit and to convince people that the Mob meant what it said. It was a reputation that everyone knew who lived and worked around Detroit during the 1960s and 70s. The Mafia had a penchant for using violence. It was casual to them, and they considered it as just 'business as usual.' Mostly, the reputation that preceded them was powerful enough to steer any business owner or manager toward making the 'right decision' in the Mob's favor.

Some people looked up to the Mafia lifestyle. Much like it was with Bonnie and Clyde, Jesse James, and other notorious outlaws in the early twentieth century. To the naïve, those who associated with the criminal lifestyle were considered folk-heroes. It seemed kind of exciting and alluring. The money, the new cars, the girls. It all seemed inviting to see their 'flashy lifestyle.' This ideology confused people, and they perceived organized crime as being a kind of Robin Hood-of the Hood.

The restaurant business was one business sector that was heavily influenced by the Mafia. You got your paycheck from your union job, then you would go out to the restaurants and lounges to celebrate your hard work on payday. The Mob took full advantage of that. It was rough for Detroit area restaurants. They had to work within the parameters that the Mob set forth. At the same time, they operated their businesses at a distance, trying to eke out a profit from a lean balance sheet. Because restaurants depended on so many companies in their daily course of business, it was close to impossible to avoid having contact with organized crime. They had to use food suppliers, linen companies, produce and beverage suppliers, and all the other services, including the garbage companies. Many of these suppliers were owned or influenced by these notorious organized crime figures.

Ken's line of work his entire life was restaurant management, so he was in the thick of it when he restarted his restaurant career in Detroit. As a restaurant manager, he had to keep the employees satisfied enough that they didn't feel they needed to join the union. I recall him often complaining about how the unions were trying to coerce his employees to join up. On the other end of the spectrum, there were the various restaurant vendors he used. Many were under pressure, and some were owned and controlled by the Mob. He was always a target in between the two sides. He was 'the management.'

Darby's Restaurant and The Purple Gang-

Since moving to Detroit in 1960, my father settled right in and doing what he had always done since he got out of the Army after World War II. Before he enlisted for the war, he was a meat cutter in a market in Boston. While in the Army, his assigned duties were to handle all the procurement and managing of the

Officers' Club and mess hall. This was the experience that catapulted him from butcher to manager for the rest of his life. He was an excellent manager for some very prestigious restaurants and hotels along the way.

'The 2400' was a first-class hotel in Washington, DC, during the early 1950s. It was just down the block from 1600 Pennsylvania Avenue, aka: 'The White House.' I was born in nearby Baltimore in 1951, and our family of five lived in a master suite inside the hotel. With three children, my brother Kenny, and my sister, Helen and me, Ken kept looking for better-paying jobs, so we moved around some.

Coming to Detroit was like starting all over again. As soon as we arrived, Ken was eager to get back to work, but all he could find was an ad for a waiter at Darby's Restaurant on 7 Mile Road and Wyoming, on the north-west side of Detroit. 'Darby's' was a trendy Jewish Style Restaurant and Kosher Deli and catered to a Jewish clientele. Dad got the waiter's job and began working there. Ken had always been a fantastic talker and sold himself well. He was a Bostonian gentleman, so his casual manner was quite likable. Within a week after they hired him as a waiter, his boss, Sam Boesky, saw there was more to him and made him general manager of Darby's. Ken would hold that position for the next eight years until 1968

Darby's was one of Detroit's foremost dining places. It wasn't just a deli, as it started out in the mid-fifties, it was an experience. It skyrocketed in popularity during the 1960s. Ken helped tremendously in building it into a favorite for all walks, which included the Mafia. It had a Skylight Lounge with live piano music, its own bakery, with 120 employees on staff and could seat 475 people at once, serving up to 5,000 guests per day. Ken Tubman was no slouch, and Sam Boesky relished the business it brought in to Darby's.

Over time, dad became more and more familiar with all the clientele. He started meeting some friends of Sam Boesky, who frequently came into Darby's for dinner. He had heard little about the 'Jewish Mafia' before. We were not from Detroit, but Ken was astute and caught on quickly about Darby's, the Purple Gang, and the Boesky brothers having some mutual affiliation in Detroit in the past. Dad always figured it was none of his business about the personal lives of other people. So, he didn't stick his nose into Sam's personal matters, and Ken enjoyed his regular paycheck and fulfilling his passion for the restaurant business.

Part of my father's job as the general manager was to negotiate the best deals from the vendors, select the best quality food items, and schedule the employees. His presence was to be out in the dining room to oversee the waiters and busboys and also greet each guest and then seat them at their table. He always made a point of learning who the regulars were and their names. Especially if they were friends of Sam's. If someone was especially important, my father would make it his responsibility to know them by name. He would use it often and treat them exceptionally well. He would seat them, then go into the kitchen and hand-deliver the order to the chef.

If a dining guest had some particular preferences about their food order, Ken would advise the chef: "so and so" was in the dining room, and here's what they would like. My father used to tell me, "You may get a hundred compliments, but that one complaint can ruin your entire day." Every so often, I have applied that to my performance. Sam Boesky genuinely cared for my dad. He made my father an honorary Rabbi, so he could bless the food as 'Kosher,' making it OK for consumption for the Jewish guests. Well, in full disclosure, Mr. Boesky may have done that for the convenience, not necessarily just because he appreciated my father. But Ken felt honored just the same and carried his yarmulke in his coat pocket. It was the eight years of Kosher food preparation that landed Ken a job offering (1974) when he needed it most.

After a few years, Sam Boesky was upgrading from his old car to a newer model and asked dad if he would like to buy his 1959 Lincoln Continental Mark IV. He would give him an exceptional deal and let him make payments from his paycheck. Dad's car was looking shabby, so he jumped at the chance to drive such a nice newer car. It was all black and had white leather upholstery with all power seats and windows. Ken always preferred the feel of driving a big roomy car. If I remember correctly, it was somewhere around 1967, so it wasn't even ten years old yet.

About a week before Ken took ownership of his Lincoln Continental Mark IV from Mr. Boesky, he was doing what he was best at. He was negotiating the best deal from one of his juice vendors, The Home Juice Company. Dad wasn't happy that they kept raising their prices and switched to a more reasonably priced juice vendor. Saving a few dollars for the restaurant was what he was good at.

Several days had passed, and dad finally got to drive his Lincoln home. It was the end of his usual twelve-hour shift on his feet all day. I know what he felt as he opened the door to the vehicle. I'm sure he appreciated the way the door felt as he opened it, it was 'solid.' As he sat on the comfortable soft white leather upholstery and started her up, he probably listened carefully to the deep sound of the V-8 engine. Ken could tell the difference between an eight-cylinder compared to a six. He must have thought he had finally arrived.

Ken headed towards home and filled it up at a nearby filling station. The attendant in those days pumped the gas for you while you sat behind the wheel. When the attendant finished pumping the gas, he walked up to dad's window and said, "You're a very lucky man, mister. Did you know there was a fuse in your gas tank? If it hadn't had fallen out, you would have blown up when you started this car."

Dad arrived home, flushed as a ghost, and shaken. It was hard for him to even get the story out as he told us all that had happened. Ken didn't know if they meant it for him, because he had changed juice companies the week before, or maybe they intended it for the former owner of the Lincoln, Sam Boesky. Dad never found out the actual reason, but it was almost a relief to think he was not the intended target. It was most likely meant for Sam Boesky, and people didn't yet know it wasn't his car any longer. I don't know if he even told Boesky about it, but I know he didn't report it to the police. Ken later learned that Home Juice company was owned by Tony and Vito Giacalone. We all know who they are. Ken was uneasy from that point on. He gave notice and left for greener and safer paths in early 1968. He concluded it was time to cash in his chips and move on.

In 1968 there were six mob-related homicides in Detroit. Some of those were car bombings. One killing was the murder of a mob wife, a 29-year-old. Her car was towed over and left behind Darby's Restaurant on Aug 18, 1968, with her lifeless body inside. It had mob undertones written all over it. Just one month before this, in July 1968, Darby's had burnt down. They shuttered it up for good. News reports had shown that they saw two cars speeding away from the trash dumpster the night it burned down. Like the Kenny Rogers song: (The Gambler), "Know when to walk away, know when to run." Whew! As I had mentioned, my dad was a perceptive man.

I didn't work for my dad until I was a senior in high school. I worked with my father as a busboy at The Rotunda Country Inn on Pine Lake Road. He knew I needed it to pay for college, and I was about to attend Eastern Michigan University over in Ypsilanti. Those were the years I grew closest to dad. I saw him every day in the summer. Before working with him, I only saw him on his one day off, which was Monday. Even then, it wouldn't be till getting home from school that we'd get to spend time with him.

Monday was his special day, and he'd like to do the cooking. It was always a roast, cooked the way it was supposed to be, but it was still much too rare for mom's liking. There would be occasional dinner flareups when Frances wanted to put ketchup on her meat. The professional 'butcher' would surface in my father and cause a family stir. "You'll ruin the meat by putting that stuff on it." She would always win the contest.

His signature late lunch dish on Monday's was what he called "Welsh Rarebit." (BTW. It's definitely not "rabbit," it's "rarebit"). It was just fancy cheese and crackers. But we loved it. As a matter of fact, I made it last night. Ken had to work every holiday, especially Mother's Day and Father's Day, Christmas and New Year, and so on. Since he only had Mondays as his day off, which was a school day, I tried to ditch school on a Monday when I was in junior high, and I wanted to stay home to be with dad. I wasn't sick. I couldn't use that as an excuse. All I could think of was I couldn't find any white socks to wear to school. We fought for an hour and a half over the socks. I won out but had to stay in my room. About forty-five minutes, anyway. I think he eventually realized it was all about being home with him, not the white socks.

The Author's Union Membership and Work Experience in Detroit- My work experience in Detroit was a little milder than my father's, but interesting, just the same. There were a lot of jobs around Detroit, but many of them meant that you had to join a union if you wanted a good wage. The Labor Unions were in full throttle during the 60s and 70s. I had my taste of working as a union member during the last six years that I was living in Michigan before I moved to California in 1976. I was in the UAW when I worked at Ford Motor, then a Teamster at UPS and Consolidated Freightways. If you wanted a job in a factory, a grocery store, or transportation, they were all dominated by the AFL/CIO or Teamsters. It was not a casual alliance, either. If you ever got caught crossing a picket line and got labeled a 'scab,' you'd better be watching your backside.

The union dues seemed to always be going up. But all the union workers I worked with weren't much concerned about what the union did with their weekly contributions. The hourly wages they got was enough to support whatever they needed for the family, so there is enough left over for whatever the union had to do. Just keep getting those pay raises for us and keep those benefits coming. BTW: Top pay in 1975 at Consolidated was $6.57/hr. Jimmy Hoffa was our demagogue. He was a virtual tough guy who got down in the trenches right along with us. The comradery was tight within the union. In my experience, the perception of being a 'tough-guy' was handed down straight from Hoffa himself. Everyone knew that if Jimmy Hoffa was on your side, you couldn't lose. Even the advertising to support and join unions was all about power and muscle. It was by use of force that the Mafia also used in its 'negotiations.'

I remember when I was offered a foreman's position at Consolidated Freightways. I was a worker on the loading dock, so I was in the union. But I knew it would be like going over to the enemy in everyone's eyes, so I turned it down. I didn't want to become 'one of them.' Going to the other side and becoming a non-union supervisor or 'manager' would be thought of as being a 'Benedict Arnold.'

Violence was always simmering between the freight-dock workers and management. You would have to make sure you were always looking over your shoulder in case you've upset somebody out there. One morning our foreman-supervisor showed up at the freight-dock with a bruised eye and would not elaborate on how it happened. One of my coworkers suggested they followed him to his car the night before. He just turned and went back into his office, lit up a cigarette, and looked at us through his window overlooking the dock.

Teamsters.org/Teamster History

"I still have the habit he drilled into me

about getting into a car.

I put my right leg in, and my left leg stays out,

and then I start my car.

If the car is rigged and you start your car that

way, you have a 50-50 chance of surviving

because if it blows up,

it will blow you out of the car."

-Jimmy Hoffa

Joe Franco, a former Hoffa lieutenant, described the security technique Hoffa taught his officers:
By Pat Zacharias / The Detroit News

2-The Mafia & The Restaurant Business

Aside from my own work experience, there is one fond memory I have from 1969 and 1970.

It was during my senior year of high school, I met a nice Italian girl from Dearborn at the Roostertail, a night club on the Detroit River. Rare Earth was the bar band, ("Get Ready" was their 1 hit wonder that went national). We dated steadily through our junior and senior years of high school. She attended Fordson High in Dearborn, and I went to Oak Park High, we both were class of '69. Oak Park was a predominantly Jewish community. Dearborn was culturally divided between Italian, Greek, and everyone else, mixed in with various Middle Eastern sections at the time. My best friend from Oak Park was Jewish and taught me a lot about his traditions and faith. One time he asked me if my girlfriend could fix him up with one of her friends from Dearborn, so we introduced him to a good friend of hers who was Syrian. The four of us went to a house party together in Dearborn. But the two of them just didn't seem to hit it off from the very start.

I really liked this girl and became very close to her and the whole family. She had two brothers and two sisters, and her grandmother lived with them as well. 'Grandma-ma' loved to cook and enjoyed impressing me with my favorite food, which happened to be Italian. So, I was treated regularly to authentic Italian cuisine, like squid, (she called them 'rubber bands'), calzone, stuffed grape leaves, and pizza bread. Her mother was divorced, and she worked at the local Wards department store in furniture sales. She was very outgoing and friendly, and she knew everybody in Dearborn, it seemed. Her mother and my mother also got along really well, and the four of us went on a few outings or dates together.

On a couple of occasions, I went with my girlfriend and her mother to visit a close family friend's house in St Clair Shores, which is on the North-East side of Detroit. I was introduced as 'the boyfriend' to Zina and then Jack. My girlfriend and I sat away from the other older adults. We enjoyed a casual lunch at our own picnic table overlooking Lake St. Clair. As we were leaving, the nice woman handed me some home-made cookies for me to take home. The next time we visited a few months later, she did exactly the same thing and gave me some more home-made cookies. Christmas cookies this time. Zina wanted me to take them back home to my mother.

Frances really liked my girlfriend's mom too. One time we went on a group date with my girlfriend, her mom, and the sweet couple we visited in St Clair Shores. We got to ride in separate limousines to see Diana Ross and the Supremes at the Fisher Theater in Detroit. It was really cool riding in a limo on a date. We rode there and back, but in separate limos. After the concert, we all stopped in a little Italian restaurant that was on the way home, and we sat at the same large table together. There were about nine or ten of us in all. I felt a bit strange when I noticed standing behind us were four or five big men in trench coats and wearing hats with their hands in their coat pockets. They were standing in a circle around us and watching us enjoying our pizza and antipasto. (Hmmm? I thought).

After the Supremes concert date, my girlfriend enlightened me on the Giacalone couple. She said there were two Giacalone brothers, Tony and Vito. But Vito was no longer in the Mafia. I didn't know you could leave the Mafia. I always thought you were either in it for life. From that time on, I remained cautiously polite in their presence. However, I was still too young and uninformed to be very worried about it. Besides, they seemed very friendly and welcoming to me.

Our moms became good friends and loved talking to each other. My mom was asked if she would like to join us for a special occasion with their friends from St. Clair Shores to celebrate their daughter's wedding. I remember it was in a banquet hall with all kinds of Italian foods laid out on the banquet tables and a band playing all Italian music. Before we sat down to eat, my girlfriend nudged me and asked if I was going to congratulate the father of the bride. I didn't know what I was going to say, but I figured the less I said, the better. So, it was a firm handshake and a quick "Congratulations, Mr. Giacalone," along with a smile back and forth between us.

When my father heard about the different outings that mom was going to with us, he said he was concerned I was being groomed or something. I assured him that wasn't the case, and I told him the same thing my girlfriend had said: "Not all Italians are in the Mafia. It's just that in a small town like Dearborn, all the Italians just know each other."

Ken Tubman turns down a desperately needed job and takes early retirement instead.

In 1974 my father was turning sixty-two. He had fallen a couple of years earlier and injured his back and was unable to stand for very long periods. At his age, finding a job was nearly impossible. Nobody needed a sixty-two-year-old restaurant manager. He had gone without work for over a year by then and losing his self-esteem over it. He ran across an ad for a general manager for a pretty elegant banquet hall over in Southfield called The Raleigh House, on Telegraph Road near 10 Mile Road. He knew something about them, and that their specialty was Kosher food preparation. It was located in a heavily Jewish area with clientele that demanded Kosher-style food. He really thought it was a perfect fit with his experience at Darby's.

Ken was desperate, but he needed this job for his self-image as well as he needed it for the income. He dressed up in his best suit, got a haircut, "both of them," as dad would say, and went for the personal interview with the owner, Sam Leiberman. Ken was given the grand tour of the kitchen facilities, which had just been remodeled. Apparently, Sam Leiberman thought it was a perfect match as well. Dad was hired on the spot, and they wanted him to start ASAP.

I spoke to him from school in Ypsilanti, and I could hear the excitement in his voice. He even sounded younger. When he told me that he had a new job, he told me a little bit about it. He said the kitchen was just remodeled and really spectacular. It was everything a meat cutter could want. It had stainless steel counters and huge band saws for butchering the meat. It had drains in the middle of the floor for the blood runoff, and it was extremely spacious. I knew my folks were having money problems and thought this would help pull them out of it.

I didn't hear this next part until my mother told me when she was living with us in Napa, California, with our family from 2007-2011. She said my dad was so proud of having the new job that he brought her over to the Raleigh House just before he was to start working there, just to show off the impressive kitchen. She said they had lunch there, and then dad showed her the kitchen. She also mentioned the stainless-steel counters and the band saws for cutting the meat. But then she added something I don't recall my dad describing. She said that there were all of these big sides of beef that were hanging on meat hooks and on rollers so they could be rolled into the big meat lockers in the kitchen.

The very next phone conversation I had with my father was why he turned the job down just a day before starting. Since the previous call, my father had spoken with a friend who had told him that The Raleigh House was owned by someone associated with the Purple Gang or the Jewish Mafia. My dad was devastated by the information. He called Mr. Leiberman and made some excuse why he could not take the job after all, and dad quit just one day before he was scheduled to start.

That seemed to be the last bit of energy he could muster up. This sucked out of him every remaining ounce of enthusiasm and pride he had left. He never worked another day in his life. He filed for early retirement in 1974, at age 62.

CHAPTER 3
Jul 30, 1975-The Machus Red Fox
Hoffa & O'Brien-Timelines

There are multiple sources for the whereabouts of Jimmy Hoffa on the day he went missing. The most straightforward timeline I could come up with follows in a simple itinerary without any disputes to footnote by using an asterisk. There is no 'Gap Alert!' There were six eyewitnesses the FBI strongly believes pinpoint the time Hoffa vanished as **2:30 pm**. Hence, I will use this as the official time, but it very well could have been as late as **2:45 pm.**

There is an asterisk regarding the **2:30;** however, a claim by Louis Linteau that would throw Hoffa's disappearance off by an hour. Why would Linteau do this, and to what end? There is no solid answer. But, because the hour is critical to the last contact with Jimmy Hoffa that afternoon, I explore that claim further a little later on.

Common knowledge tells us the reasons for the all-important meeting which Jimmy Hoffa was anxiously anticipating for **2:00 pm** on Wednesday at The Machus Red Fox. Just days before the scheduled session, there was a get together on July 26, 1975. That meeting was held at Hoffa's Lake Orion home with both Tony and his brother Vito Giacalone. The primary topic was to smooth things over with Tony Provenzano and make the road to regain the union presidency a smoother path for Hoffa. In retrospect, that strategy meeting was the setup for Hoffa to feel like

Provenzano wanted to make amends so he could proceed to the 1976 campaign.

JOSEPH ZIRILLI-Detroit mob Boss: The Hoffa hit would have to have Joe Zirillis' prior approval.

In February of 1975, there was a meeting between Joe Zirilli, Tony Giacalone, Billy Giacalone (Vito), along with Peter Vitale and Jimmy Quasarano, both co-owners of Central Sanitation. The 'Hoffa Hit' would have had to have been approved by Mafia Boss, Joseph Zirilli, so it would not be done without his OK. This may have been the meeting where Zirilli gave the OK to go forward.

Jimmy Hoffa was getting pretty friendly with the feds, and the news was getting around about it. He had some dirt on Fitzsimmons' union activities, and he was about to unleash it as a bargaining chip to remove the union restrictions placed against him by Nixon. Everyone knew it, Chuckie O'Brien was also busy spreading the word among Mafia notables that Hoffa was a snitch and planned to rat out the Mafia. Hoffa was also turning down mob requests for pension money and loans. There were previous plans instigated before this to take Hoffa out of the picture, but they fizzled. This time would be different.

The 2:00 pm meeting with Tony Giacalone, Tony Provenzano, and Leonard Schultz was not intended to take place inside the Red Fox, but at another nearby location. The Red Fox had a dress code (Coat and tie), and Hoffa was not dressed for it. Witnesses claim he went inside looking for the others after waiting a short time outside the restaurant.

James Riddle Hoffa - Wednesday-July 30, 1975

AM - Hoffa's residence in Lake Orion, Michigan

Jimmy Hoffa awoke early and was anxious about the **2 pm** meeting. Has breakfast with his wife, Josephine, did a crossword puzzle and took a cat-nap on the picnic table. As he is leaving for the Red Fox meeting, Jimmy tells Jo that he'll be home by **4:00** and will grill some steaks for dinner.

1:00 pm - It's 40 Miles from his home to The Machus Red Fox-Stops briefly at ASL, Pontiac.

Hoffa gets into his 1974 Pontiac Grand Ville and leaves for the meeting at the Red Fox.

1:30 pm - 200 North Paddock, Pontiac, MI/Airport Service Lines-Limo Service

Hoffa stops to see Louis Linteau at ASL (Owned by Louis Linteau). Linteau is out to lunch. Hoffa talks with Elmer Reeves and others. He leaves a message about the Red Fox meeting w/Tony Giacalone, Tony Provenzano, and Leonard Schultz.

2:00 pm - 6676 Telegraph Road, Bloomfield Twp., MI/The Machus Red Fox Restaurant

Hoffa arrives precisely at **2:00 pm**. He waits outside briefly, then goes inside the restaurant and speaks with several people. Still, there was no sign of Tony Giacalone, Tony Provenzano, or Leonard Schultz.

2:15 pm - Hoffa is seen by witnesses making calls

Jimmy Hoffa makes two phone calls from the payphone at Dammon Hardware behind the restaurant. He calls his wife,

Josephine, and is really upset about the "No-shows' to the meeting, and tells her he's coming home now to grill the steaks. Then he makes another call.

2:35 - Hoffa calls LINTEAU at ASL and tells about the no-shows. (Confirmed)

***2:30-2:45 pm** -**Several eyewitnesses had seen Hoffa between**
2:00   and 2:45 pm

Five of them shook Jimmy Hoffa's hand. 1 more witness sees him at the pay-phone. Another sees him get into the Mercury with three other men. Still, another witness is driving a delivery truck and sees him in the rear seat as the Mercury is leaving. The delivery truck almost collides with the car as it exits and turns south onto Telegraph Road.

* 'GAP Alert!'

***3:30** - LINTEAU**

Gave an alternate time for the call to ASL from Hoffa.

July 30 - Later that night: 10:00 pm

Hoffa's wife, Josephine, begins to make calls when Jimmy doesn't show up at the house.

-Calls JOSEPH BANE SR-friend and another Teamster Official.

-Calls her son-JAMES HOFFA JR. who was on vacation in Traverse City, MI.

-Calls daughter-Barbara Ann Crancer, who was living in St Louis, MO.

-LOUIS LINTEAU Calls Josephine from ASL at **10 pm.**

Louis Linteau makes other calls from ASL at 10pm.

After Linteau calls Mrs. Hoffa, he makes more calls.

-Calls JOSEPH BANE, who he was with earlier in the evening.

-Calls TONY GIACALONE, who was at Joey Giacalone's apartment.

-Calls CYNTHIA GREEN, which is his ASL business associate. He asks her to meet him at the Hoffa residence. They both stay the night and for the week. In testimony, Mrs. Hoffa said Linteau did not make a single call in search of Hoffa the entire time he stayed at her house all week. This would indicate Linteau was not genuinely interested in the whereabouts of Jimmy Hoffa.

Author's Notes-

The FBI said - Six witnesses saw Hoffa at The Red Fox Restaurant between **2:00 and 2:45 pm**. More witnesses agreed with the **2:30** time estimate. But a fifteen-minute window stretches that out to **2:45 pm**.

-*Witness: (Un-named)* A retired Real Estate broker and another with him shakes Hoffa's hand in the Red Fox Parking Lot. The witness does not want his real name revealed for fear of reprisal from the Mafia.

-*Witness:* Sees Jimmy Hoffa using the payphone at **2:20** behind getting into the maroon   Mercury with 3 other men, sat in the back seat behind the driver. Hoffa is leaning forward and gesturing with his hands at the driver as though he were arguing with him.

-*Witness:* A delivery truck driver is entering the same driveway, as the Mercury and has to veer out of the way to avoid colliding with the car as it is pulling out of the side driveway. It then turns right onto Telegraph Road heading South. He recognizes Jimmy Hoffa was seated in back on the driver's side. He spots a gray blanket and what appears to be a shotgun lying on the rear bench seat between Hoffa and the other man also seated in the back. 2 men were sitting in front.

* 'GAP Alert'!

A 'Gap Alert'! Means it was related to the **2:30 to 3:30 pm** period on July 30, 1975.

*3:30 - **LINTEAU gave an alternate time for the call to ASL from Jimmy Hoffa.**

However, the claim was disproven by actual phone records and by the person who was on the phone with Linteau when Hoffa's call was announced as being on the other line, at **2:35 pm**.

2:30-2:45 pm- This was the most consistent with all of the eyewitnesses when Hoffa was taken away from the Machus Red Fox Restaurant. The latest time edges towards **2:45 pm**.

Hoffa made 2 consecutive calls from the pay-phone at Dammon Hardware

Hoffa called his wife at 2:15 pm. Right after he hung up, he made another call to Airport Service Lines and spoke with the owner, Louis Linteau. Evidence shows that call was made at precisely 2:35 pm. (Michigan Bell phone records & Thomas Carson confirm).

Hoffa spurned need for guard

DETROIT (AP) — "The only guy who needs a body-guard is a liar, a cheat, a guy who betrays friendship," ex-Teamsters President James R. Hoffa said a month before he disappeared July 30.

"I don't need any of them."

In a copyright interview published in the December issue of Playboy magazine, the former union boss defended his longtime acquaintance Anthony "Tony Jack" Giacalone, a reputed Mafia figure who has been a central figure in the federal probe of Hoffa's disappearance.

The tape-recorded interview was conducted in June by Jerry Stanecki, a radio newsman in Detroit.

Hoffa said in the interview that Giacalone was "a businessman" who had been unfairly hounded by the government on tax matters.

Giacalone was one of three men the ex-union boss apparently believed he was on his way to meet the afternoon of the day he vanished.

Giacalone's alibi for July 30 is that he was at the Southfield Athletic Club and never knew of any scheduled meeting with Hoffa. Giacalone is under indictment for tax evasion.

On that issue, Hoffa said, "They take you from the time you got outta school until now, ask people how much you've spent, add up your salary — and they just put it on you and the law says you have to disprove it. That's what Giacalone's gotta prove now.

"They put a net worth on him and now Giacalone's gotta restructure his whole life from the time he was born to show where he got his money. It's gonna be a hell of a thing to do."

Asked about reputed mobsters he has known, Hoffa retorted, "I don't believe there is any organized crime, period. Don't believe it. Never believed it. I've said it for the last 40 years."

Asked if he ever hired bodyguards, he said, "Never. Don't need 'em ... They're in your way ... You got a bodyguard, you become careless, and if you look at all the gangsters that were killed with bodyguards, you'll know they went to sleep. I don't care to go to sleep."

Asked if he had ever ordered anybody killed, Hoffa paused and said, "Mmm, nope." He added: "Killing isn't the way to solve a problem."

James Hoffa

corpus christi

TIMES

P.O. Box 9136
Corpus Christi, Texas, 78408

Published each weekday afternoon except Saturday at 820 N. Lower Broadway, Corpus Christi, Texas by the Caller-Times Publishing Co. Second class postage paid at Corpus Christi, Texas

Robert C. Dorsey .... Business Manager
Clarence Trafton .... Circulation Manager
J. Roy Daniel .... Production Manager
Andy L. Scheopf .... Adv. Sales Manager
James J. Weston .... Personnel Manager
Charles F. Leach .... Creative Director
Kenneth D. Holt .... Controller

Member of The Associated Press. The Associated Press is entitled exclusively to the use for publication of all local news printed in this newspaper as well as all AP news dispatches.

SUBSCRIPTION RATES
MAIL RATES INCLUDING TAX: Morning, evening and Sunday, 12 months $67.84, 6 months $43.92, 3 months $21.96. Morning or evening and Sunday, 12 months $60.04, 6 months $31.27, 3 months $15.68. Morning or evening only, 12 months $48.00, 6 months $24.00, 3 months $12.20. Sunday only, 12 months $39.90, 6 months $18.43, 3 months $9.74.

CARRIER RATES INCLUDING TAX: Morning, evening and Sunday, 12 months $79.56, 6 months $39.78, 3 months $19.89, 1 month $6.62, 1 week $1.53. Morning or evening and Sunday, 12 months $58.68, 6 months $29.34, 3 months $14.67, 1 month $4.89, 1 week $1.13.

Bodyguards: "Never. Don't need 'em. They're in your way. You got a bodyguard, you become careless."
Jimmy Hoffa-Playboy Magazine-1975

Chuckie O'Brien's whereabouts are ambiguous and everchanging-

I endeavored to make this first O'Brien timeline as simplified as I could. The most difficult challenge was trying to insert accurate times and places for Mr. O'Brien. Even if you take Chuckie at his word, (did I just say that?). I wondered, Should I use his initial claims, or go by his additions and recanting of previous claims?

Maybe I should just ignore everything he said entirely? I elected to consider all statements. If he made a statement and then changed it in a subsequent interview, I reasoned how the change would affect other statements. I also considered that if a particular time or place was changed or recanted, then I must adjust the other items of the timeline e accordingly. When O'Brien said he did NOT go to the Southfield Athletic Club, I moved everything else in his itinerary back to suit that time slot.

The FBI gave reasons for having such extreme difficulty in assembling their own timeline, had to do with the vast discrepancies in what O'Brien said. He would provide them with a specific time, then in the same interview, change it. His arrival and departure times overlapped and given as guesses or estimates. But the multiplicity of times and locations were exceedingly difficult to keep track of.

The other major problem noted by agents was that the only witnesses who were even willing to speak were primarily those who were also the main suspects. (O'Brien, Linteau and so on). All of the other primary suspects said nothing. They pled the fifth, refusing to speak at all (Tony Giacalone, Tony Provenzano, etc.).

I paid a fair amount of attention to several of the other peripheral witnesses that gave an interview to the FBI. There were various additional informants who either confirmed or contradicted the main characters and their claims. There was a secretary, multiple employees, or other uninvolved persons who had some further observations. But more importantly, there were six eyewitnesses mentioned with varying details that were included in the HOFFEX report. Some of their comments caught my attention because they echoed Ken and Frances Tubman's details.

I had no foregone conclusions, so I took everything in at face value. Some things were trivial and not worth lying about. Maybe that's what draws attention. Why did O'Brien think he must lie about it? My focus was more on 'The Gap' or the 60-minutes between **2:30 and 3:30 pm.**

Charles Lenton O'Brien - Wednesday-July 30, 1975
The Morning-

Chuckie O'Brien's daily routine was very consistent. He would be dropped off at The Machus Red Fox each morning by Marvin Adell, whom he has lived with since his divorce. Then he is picked up at the Red Fox soon after by Robert Holmes Jr., who transports O'Brien to the Trumbull office for work. This would have been the typical daily routine for Chuckie O'Brien for this day as well. But it was not so typical in the afternoon

There was also something else that was out of the ordinary about this particular Wednesday, July 30, 1975. He had been booked on a flight to Toronto-At the last minute, O'Brien decided not to go. He said, "It would be a waste of time to go," because

he had to pack and get ready for the transfer to Miami by
Fitzsimmons. It must have been a sudden change. Holmes
mentioned to the FBI that he waited at the Detroit Metro Airport
for him to show, but he never did.

O'Brien calls Robert Holmes Jr. for a ride at **7:45 am**, which
indicates it was not a previously arranged ride as a typical day
would have been.

7:45 am- O'Brien calls Holmes Jr., tells him he's not going to
Toronto, after all, and needs a ride to work. Adell drops COB
off at the Machus Red Fox parking lot, and Holmes Jr. picks
him up and takes him to Trumbull-arriving at **9:30 am**. During
the morning, he is packing his belongings for the upcoming
transfer to Miami union offices.

9:30 am- Local #299 Offices: 2801 Trumbull Avenue Detroit
Chuckie is dropped off at Trumbull by Robert Holmes, Jr.

11:45 am- Delivery of fresh 16 lb. Coho Salmon
The package is signed for by CAROL DAVIS, a teamster
employee. O'Brien tells the FBI (Aug 6 int) that He was the
one who signed for it. Then Chuckie volunteers to deliver the
salmon to Robert Holmes, a fellow union member in
Farmington Hills, MI. COB had no means to deliver the
Salmon to Holmes. So, he asks to borrow Joey Giacalone's car,
a brand new 1975 maroon Mercury Marquis Brougham sedan.
Joey agrees and brings it over. When O'Brien is asked why he
didn't just use the union station wagon in the parking lot, he
said he could not locate the keys.

12:00 Noon- 2801 Trumbull Ave-Local 299 in Detroit.

Chuckie gets the Mercury from Joey Giacalone, puts the Salmon behind the driver's seat, then drops Joey Giacalone back at his place of business in St. Clair Shores and heads to the Holmes residence in Farmington Hills, Michigan.

12:50 pm- Holmes Residence: 36045 Congress Court- Farmington Hills, MI. 36 miles/35-minute drive time- O'Brien arrives at the Holmes residence, helps Mrs. Holmes cut up the salmon into steaks. COB later mentions he made two calls from Holmes. One to Tony Giacalone, who was busy getting a rub down. The second call was to Marvin Adell.

2:20 pm- *(Approximate time).* COB claims to have gone to Jax Kar Wash and asked the attendants to "Clean the fish blood out before it starts to stink."

2:40 pm- Jax to Lift-All is 30.4 miles/30-minute drive time. O' Brien claims he left Jax at **2:40 pm**. After figuring in the changes he made to the alibi, the only other stop would have been Lift-All on Conner to return the Mercury back to Joey Giacalone. (60-minute Gap)

4:00 pm- LIFT-ALL/2679 Conner Street, Detroit, MI (Lift-All/Joey Giacalone's business) Joey Giacalone said O'Brien arrived at Lift-All between **3:30 and 4:00.**

4:30 pm- 2801 Trumbull Ave, Detroit, MI/Local #299- 7.6 miles/10-minute drive time.

O'Brien is dropped off at **4:30 pm**. Based on the actual distance and drive time, and O'Brien was seen at **4:30 pm.** The more accurate time is **4:30** (Per Joey Giacalone himself).

Author's Notes-

Using Chuckie O'Brien's own claims, after all of his changes and recantations have been applied, Chuckie's timeline should look like the following:

-Trumbull to Holmes (Left **12:00 noon**)

-Holmes to Jax Kar Wash (Left at **2:20 pm**)

-Jax Kar Wash to Conner-Joey G. (Left at **2:40pm**)

 (Arrived at **4:00 pm**)

-Trumbull Offices **(4:30)**

* 'GAP Alert'!

There's *STILL* a 60-90-minute time gap every way you look at it. O'Brien's alibi will be delved into more thoroughly in Chapter 7.

RE: Alibi Changes:

Changes in the alibis by Chuckie O'Brien and a lack of support for his various explanations, makes O'Brien's timeline appear confusing at first. But the FBI conducted several hours of interviews with O'Brien, and they simulated the best-case scenarios.

The agents tested all variations of the alibi over several months. Every one of them had ended up with a 60 to a 90-minute gap in time, saying that O'Brien "Cannot account for his time between **2:30 and 3:30 pm**," regardless of which scenario they used. (HOFFEX)

CHAPTER 4-Part I
July 30, 1975-The Family Secret
The Tubman Timeline

Now, I offer you a third timeline.

One that you have *NEVER* seen before.

Some terrific timelines have been published by several authors and investigative reporters. I don't make any attempts to conflict with those offered by the host of experts who has provided excellent accounts of the whereabouts of Jimmy Hoffa and Chuckie O'Brien. Yet there is one timeline no one else has been able to offer, the Tubman timeline.

In the timelines just presented, I primarily derived the claims used from those statements provided in the HOFFEX memo. Then I tried to reconstruct what I believe to be true to Chuckie O'Brien's own words. His initial times that were given, the changes he made to those times, and finally, the changes resulting from his ultimate recanting of previous claims.

With this third and final itinerary, I endeavored to adhere to my own initial premise and worked outward from there. I began with what Ken and Frances saw during that period. You must consider that no-one else has been privy to these details.

The Tubmans were never mentioned in the news media. They were not even mentioned in the thousands of pages of FBI documentation. That is because they were never formal witnesses. Ken and Frances were never subpoenaed to testify before the Federal Grand Jury in Detroit. Therefore, their names will not appear anywhere else but here. No other timelines will include their story because, except for the FBI in 2006 and a few select individuals since then, the secret has remained hidden from the eyes of the general public.

Regarding the previous Hoffa and O'Brien timelines, serious questions remain. If the Tubman timeline provides an overlapping of events and is consistent with what the other eyewitnesses claimed, then you can trust it for accuracy. After all, I heard the details well <u>before</u> it was printed in headlines and broadcast on the news. The specific information fills in the gaps that were left by the other timelines.

Besides the 60-minute 'Gap,' there is still much more to discover during the days leading up to, and the days that follow Hoffa's disappearance. But for the purposes of this book, the focus will be on the **2:30-3:30** period. Remember the caveat at the beginning of the book? You need to shelve whatever forgone conclusions you held on to before this, and believe as I do. I've told you more about the Tubmans, so I hope you feel you know them a lot better now. Hopefully, you know them enough to trust them, and agree that there is no reason to doubt their account.

<u>Kenneth & Frances Tubman- Wednesday-July 30, 1975</u>

My parents, Kenneth and Frances Tubman, were renting a two-story townhome at Bloomfield Terrace, which was a townhome complex at 36643 Woodward Avenue. It was part of Bloomfield Township back then. It was situated on Woodward Avenue, between Maple or 15 Mile and 16 Mile Roads. Ken and Frances Tubman had made plans with their daughter, Helen

Kersten, to enjoy a camp-over with her family. The Kersten's had a new Coleman pop-up camper and thought it would be fun for the family to go to the lake with it for a couple of nights. So, Ken and Frances were packing for the two-night campout during the morning and early afternoon. Although I was living with them at the time, I did not join them.

They planned to leave by **2:00 or 2:15** to make it to Helen's by **4:00 pm.** They had it timed so that they would not have to rush if they were to leave home by then. That gave them ample time to drive the hour and twenty minutes to Helen's place. Both Ken and Frances were retired, so watching the clock was generally approximated by fifteen-minute intervals.

Ken would be driving, and Frances sat next to the front passenger seat window, which would have been rolled down since it was 91 degrees that day, and there was no air-conditioner in the car.

They took the usual route to Helen's, who lived at 30816 Grandview in Westland. They usually drove down Woodward Avenue to Maple (15 Mile Road), turn right, and go over to Telegraph Road. That's the intersection where the Machus Red Fox Restaurant was situated within a little strip center in the same town they lived in, Bloomfield Township. After turning onto Telegraph Road, heading south, they would continue on Telegraph all the way down to Michigan Avenue, turn right and go over to Helen's place in Westland. My father was one of those drivers that always preferred to drive in the left lane. So, right after his turn onto Telegraph Road from Maple, he hugged the far-left hand lane, as usual.

Tubman Residence: 36643 Woodward Avenue, Bloomfield Township *Morning-*

Kenneth and Frances Tubman were busy preparing for a two-night camping trip with their daughter's family, The Kersten's. They packed all morning long and into the early afternoon and placed their things into their car for the drive to Helen's. All intentions were to leave home by **2:15** to get to Westland by **4:00 pm**. They came within 15-minutes of the plan.

2:15 to 2:30 pm-

Ken and Frances leave their residence and head southbound on Woodward Avenue. Turning right onto Maple Road (aka 15 Mile Road), then turn left onto Telegraph Road.

2:30 to 2:45 pm-

Ken and Frances are passing by the east-side driveway of the Red Fox. At that moment, a big maroon-colored car hastily exited from the driveway. Frances noticed it right away because of the way it veered out from the driveway and immediately pulled up tightly behind them and into the same lane, which was on the far left. The maroon vehicle pulls alongside, next to Frances for several minutes, and both cars drive even with each other down Telegraph Road.

The driver is recognized by Ken Tubman, so he tells Frances to quit looking back at him. He tells her: "Frances, stop looking at that car, That's the Mafia. Do you want to end up in the Detroit River?" But Frances can't help but look because there were two big men in the rear seat of the car, and they were violently struggling with something they were holding down on the floorboard.

2:45-3:00 pm-

The maroon car pulls ahead and makes a left as it crosses through the center divider. It pulls into a well-known restaurant on the opposite side of Telegraph Road. The Tubmans wonder why the driver was glaring at them, so they slowly pass by, and they see the car come to a full stop. They notice something else unusual in the parking lot. Confused by the events they just witnessed, they continue on to Helen's house while chatting to each other as to what it was all about and why the driver was so interested in them.

4:00 pm- (Or sooner)

They arrived at their daughter's house in Westland close to **4:00 pm**. (Per daughter, Helen Kersten).

Wednesdady July 30, 1975
Tubman-Route Driven

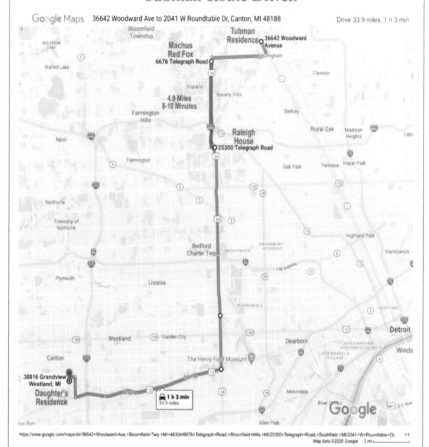

Tubmans left residence 2:15 pm to Red Fox: 4.8 mi/15 min drive time Passing Red Fox approx 2:30-2:45 pm.
Continued from Red Fox to Raleigh House: 5 mi/10 min drive time.
Raleigh House to Daughter's residence: 23.9 mi/45 min drive time. (Arrived approx. 4:00 pm).
Allowing for approximated residence departure time of 15 minutes +-.
Tubman's daughter confirms arrival time at close to 4:00 pm.

REFER TO: *The full story retold in a phone call*
I had with Frances Tubman just before the FBI interview In

May 2006

Beginning in Chapter 5

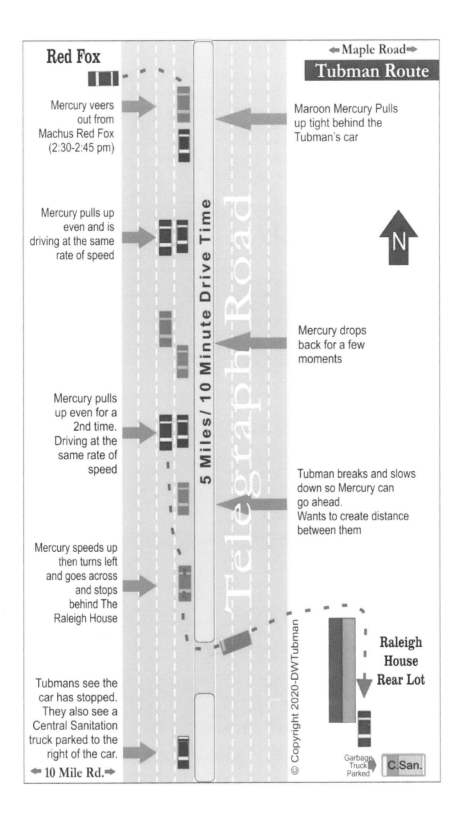

Red Fox

← Maple Road →

Tubman Route

Mercury veers out from Machus Red Fox (2:30-2:45 pm)

Maroon Mercury Pulls up tight behind the Tubman's car

Mercury pulls up even and is driving at the same rate of speed

N

Mercury drops back for a few moments

Mercury pulls up even for a 2nd time. Driving at the same rate of speed

Tubman breaks and slows down so Mercury can go ahead. Wants to create distance between them

Mercury speeds up then turns left and goes across and stops behind The Raleigh House

Raleigh House Rear Lot

Tubmans see the car has stopped. They also see a Central Sanitation truck parked to the right of the car.

Garbage Truck Parked

C.San.

← 10 Mile Rd. →

5 Miles/ 10 Minute Drive Time

Telegraph Road

© Copyright 2020-DWTubman

CHAPTER 4-Part II
"Jimmy Hoffa Is Missing"
August 1, 1975-The Realization

The First Newspaper Headlines: August 1, 1975 -

Detroit Free Press-Metro Edition

In retrospect, I had placed very little emphasis on 'The Family Secret' back in 1975. Over time the 'Hoffa Story' was hardly mentioned amongst family members anymore. But little by little, my research gave me more insight into what was known and what was still missing.

I began to see how historically significant the details my parents knew about would have mattered. It contained critical information that provides the answers to many open questions surrounding the Hoffa case. I found nothing else had touched on the very details Ken and Frances gave. Several facts still need to be exposed to clarify the events surrounding Hoffa's disappearance.

My parents were headed over to my sister's house that day. But for some reason, it never dawned on me to just call and ask Helen what she may recall about it. Just a few months ago, I had the notion of calling her in Michigan, and I brought up the 'Hoffa Story' with her. It had been forty-five years since we had first heard the account directly from our parents. For some reason, we never thought of comparing notes about the family secret until that phone call in February, just a few months ago. After the conversation, I was prompted to assemble it into this book. As we discussed the events, I realized that Helen saw some of the very first reactions that our parents had when the news first hit on August 1, 1975.

When I brought up the subject, Helen seemed to think she wouldn't remember much about it, "It was so long ago." But, as we spoke, she began to recall some things which I had not heard from her before. I always wondered what the occasion was for them visiting her that day. Helen told me about the two-night camping trip to Pinkney, which I never knew. She said that during the camping trip, her attention was primarily focused on her 18-month-old, Dawn. Helen told me what happened when mom and dad arrived at her home around **4:00 pm** that day. The more we talked, the more details she recalled.

When Ken and Frances first arrived at Helen's house at **4:00** on July 30, 1975, the three of them were chatting a bit before Helen's husband was due to get home from work. He regularly got home at **5:00.** Frances described the exciting drive she and dad had on the way over to her house. Mom was anxious and wondering out loud, "Why was that driver so interested in us? Why would he be glaring at us and the car?" She described to Helen about the two cars riding right next to each other as they came down Telegraph. But she couldn't get over all that commotion going on in the back seat. Since dad told her the Mafia was in the car and told her to quit looking, it made her even more curious about it. But the answers escaped them and just weren't coming into focus. They had no idea that in a day or so, they would get more answers than they bargained for. At the time, it seemed like idle chit chat but became memorable soon after.

Friday: Aug 1, 1975-

Helen went on to describe the two nights of the camping trip to the lake in Pinkney. They got there before dark Wednesday night, Jul 30, then relaxed the following day, which was Thursday. On Friday morning of Aug 1, it was still early as they were starting to pack up the Coleman camper to head back home. Helen had just stepped out of the camper to check on her little girl in the playpen. She saw that my dad had already picked up the morning paper. It was folded in half on the tray table outside right next to the door. All that she could see was the second half of the headlines in big, bold letters:

"- - - - - Hoffa Is Missing."

Mom and dad were seated a short distance away from her, but she could faintly hear them talking to each other, kind of briskly but quietly. She heard them asking each other questions. Ken was continuing their conversation and asked Frances: "Well, what do you think we saw?" Frances answered him: "I don't know, a big dog or something?" Ken responded: "That was no dog."

Dad seemed to already know more about what they saw, but Helen didn't relate it to what was on the headline. My sister said she was mainly thinking about her child and busy packing up, so she "kind of sluffed it off." They headed back to Helen's, then my parents drove back home from there.

Meanwhile, I was home at Bloomfield Terrace when they arrived early afternoon.

Instead of a normal "Hi, how are you," after being away for the two days, Frances seemed anxious to get to the TV and turned on the news. I was in the living room at the time with them. Mom settled onto the couch but leaned forward so she could hear, and dad preferred to stand. It must have already been in progress, but what stood out in my mind was that right as the newscaster had said, "Hoffa was last seen at The Machus Red Fox Restaurant." Then I heard my dad immediately fire back in a loud, angry voice:

"Like Hell! We saw him at The Raleigh House!"

1975 Maroon Mercury Marquis Broughm Sedan — Jimmy Hoffa seen in Rear Seat

Joey Giacalone's 1975 Mercury Marquis Brougham

I thought about it as I continued listening to them and the news. Still, I didn't sense any extreme urgency about which restaurant it was during the newscast. I just figured they made a little glitch in their reporting and got the name of the restaurant wrong. It was no big deal. But my parents seemed to be even more intently listening to the rest of the news from that point. Dad continued being emphatic about seeing Hoffa at the Raleigh House, not just the Red Fox. I didn't have any inkling what-so-ever that my mother and father had been eyewitnesses to anything unusual. I don't think the news report was playing it up as much as my folks were. I think I settled in on the notion that Hoffa was missing, but he'll turn up, I thought.

I asked for more information about it, and mom and dad were both very eager to get the story out. One would say something, then the other added a bit more, back and forth. I eventually got all the details, and over the coming days, it seemed to be the dominant discussion between the two of them.

One thing I will not forget upon hearing it for the first time was the fear I saw in their faces and the nervous tone of their voices as they told me all about it. I listened to them retell the events for several days after it happened. My father was absolutely certain he knew who the driver of the car was. He was definitely familiar with the place they went to after leaving The Machus Red Fox. He almost went to work there in 1974 but changed his mind upon learning who owned it.

Several days later, when the news started to air a picture of the man who they suspected was driving the car that Hoffa was last seen in, I heard my mother say, "That's the guy! That's the man I saw driving that big car!" Up until that point, she only knew him as the man that Ken said he had recognized. She had never heard his name before dad mentioned it in the car. Until the picture was made public, Frances had described him as a portly man with a big round head and face, with a receding hairline, and he had big long sideburns.

She also mentioned what the driver was wearing. She said he wasn't wearing a suit, like the other two men in the back. He was wearing a white shirt with a high collar. He wasn't wearing a jacket.

The two vehicles were just feet apart side by side and driving at the same rate of speed. Not only once, but twice during the short drive together. The windows in my parent's vehicle would have been rolled down as they had no air conditioning, and it was about 90 degrees. The Mercury would have likely had their windows rolled up, with the A/C going. The driver was alone in the front seat, and two men in the back were seated a little bit apart from each other. (Notice the hump in the photo below?).

Frances saw a lot of commotion going on, and both men in the back had their knees pushed high up into their chests as they were vigorously struggling with something that was on the floor. One man was holding a strap or a rope of some kind like he was trying to tie something up. But whatever was down there just wasn't cooperating. Frances envisioned because it looked like he was holding a leash, it must be a dog. They were big men too, so it must have been a big dog down there on the floorboard. It had to be something big to cause all that ruckus. After seeing the newspaper headlines, dad was more pragmatic about what was actually on the floorboard, remembering his comment, "That was no dog!"

When I think back to that original news cast, and as I was watching my parent's reactions to the news about Hoffa being missing, something didn't quite connect. My parents were treating the news far more seriously than the newscaster seemed to be. Now I believe that disparity had to do with the difference in perspective.

My father and mother KNEW the fate of Jimmy Hoffa, while the news was only speculating about him being a missing person.

Google Map Plotting: Plot for yourself

CHUCKIE O'BRIEN'S ROUTE: In his own words.

12:00 noon

-Local #299/O'Brien's Offices: 2801 Trumbull Avenue-

-Lift-All/Joey Giacalone's work: 2679 Conner Street
  Detroit, MI.

-Robert 35/46/ Residence: 36045 Congress Court-
  Farmington Hills, MI.

2:40 pm

-*Jax Kar Wash: 31500 Grand River Avenue-
  Farmington Hills, MI.

-*Southfield Athletic Club: 26555 Evergreen Road-
  Southfield, MI.

-Lift-All/Joey Giacalone's work: 2679 Conner Street-

-Local #299/O'Brien's Offices: 28011 Trumbull Avenue-
  Detroit, MI.

4:30 pm

O'Brien's Route-Overlaps the Tubman's Route: 2:30-4:00 pm

-From Machus Red Fox to Raleigh House **2:30-2:45pm**
  (3:00 latest)

2:30 pm

-Machus Red Fox Restaurant: 6676 Telegraph Road-
  Bloomfield Township, MI

-The Raleigh House: 25300 Telegraph Road-Southfield, MI

-Lift-All/Joey Giacalone's work: 2679 Conner Street-

-Local #299/O'Brien's Offices: 2801 Trumbull Avenue-

4:00 pm

TUBMAN'S ROUTE: They saw what they saw.

From 2:15 to 4:00 pm (From residence to daughter's house)

2:15 pm

-Ken and Frances Tubman-Residence: 36643 Woodward Avenue- Bloomfield Twp., MI

-Machus Red Fox Restaurant: 6676 Telegraph Road-Bloomfield Township, MI

-The Raleigh House: 25300 Telegraph Road-Southfield, MI

-Kerstens/Tubman Daughter's Residence: 30816 Grandview, Westland, MI

4:00 pm

* 'GAP Alert'!

- (Falls within the **2:30-3:30** time span)

-Jax Kar Wash: All known evidence points to O'Brien may not have gone to Jax as he claims.

-Southfield Athletic: O'Brien said he went there/changed claim, then said he "Didn't go there."

Wednesday July 30, 1975
O'Briens-Claimed Route Driven

Google Maps   36045 Congress Court, Farmington Hills, MI to 2679 Conner Street, Detroit, MI   Drive 33.7 miles, 42 min

https://www.google.com/maps/dir/36045+Congress+Court,+Farmington+Hills,+MI/31500+Grand+River+Avenue,+Farmington,+MI/2679+Conner+Street,+Detroit,+MI/@42.3949379,-83.1262415,11.94z/...   1/1

Holmes to Jax: 3.3 mi/8 min drive time. Jax to Lift-All-(Joey G.): 30.4 mi/34 min drive time. Total Mi 33.7/42 min drive time.
Leaving Holmes at 2:20pm and arriving Lift-All at 4:00 pm gave O'Brien 1 hr 40 min.
Time unaccounted for = 60 minutes.

O'Briens-Actual Route Driven Based on all evidence

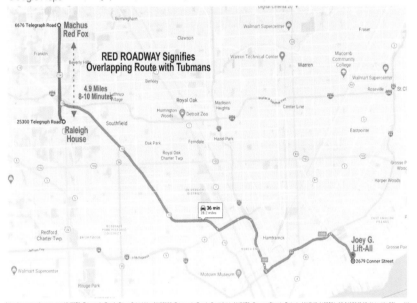

Google Maps   6676 Telegraph Road, Bloomfield Hills, MI to 2679 Conner Street, Detroit, MI   Drive 28.2 miles, 36 min

https://www.google.com/maps/dir/6676+Telegraph+Road,+Bloomfield+Hills,+MI/25300+Telegraph+,+Road,+Southfield,+MI/2679+Conner+Street,+Detroit,+MI/@42.442521,-83.0402046,12z/data=!4m20!...   1/1

Machus Red Fox: 2:30-2:45 pm: to Raleigh House 4.9 mi/80-10 min drive time. (2:40-2:55 pm arrival time)
Raleigh House to Lift-All: 23.3 mi/26 min drive time. (arrived time 4:00 pm)
Time unaccounted for = 30 minutes.

4-II-Jimmy Hoffas Is Missing-The Realization

THERE IS A TIME TO BE TOUGH
A TIME TO BE ADAMANT
A TIME TO BE OPEN TO COMPROMISE
AND A TIME TO REACH AGREEMENT

JAMES R. HOFFA
TEAMSTERS UNION PRESIDENT 1957-1971

"To the best of my recollection,

I must recall on my memory,

I cannot remember."

Jimmy Hoffa

CHAPTER 5
FBI Detroit Field Office
June 27, 2006-Frances Tubman-Ward/FBI Interview

2006 was the year that everything began to resurface regarding Jimmy Hoffa's disappearance and the family story my mom and dad had told us long ago. Since my father's passing in 1987, my mother was living alone in the same apartment they had shared at Willow Creek apartments in Westland, Michigan, just outside of Detroit. She handled it sufficiently enough that she could retain her independence and not have to move into a nursing home. She had periodic health issues, but my sister Helen lived nearby and was usually available to help mom out when needed.

Frances turned 89 in March of that year, but she was still the persistent one. She had undergone kidney surgery for the removal of the one that was cancerous. She also suffered a heart attack and a stroke, but she had fully recovered. In addition to that, Frances now had high blood pressure, diabetes, hearing aids, and age-related macular degeneration. She was legally blind, yet she drove herself to the store regularly just to get out.

AP News May 19, 2006: Hundreds of FBI agents dig up McMaster's Farm.

I was actively working in my sign business out of my home in Napa, California. As I was enjoying a morning cup of coffee before a job, I opened up the Napa Register. I immediately noticed a full-color picture and the accompanying article about hundreds of FBI agents digging up a farm in Milford Township, Michigan. I thought to myself, "They are still looking for Jimmy Hoffa's remains"? It had been so long since I even thought about it, but I was surprised. Then again, not really. It just wasn't something I kept tabs on. But I was wondering if my folks ever did tell the police or the FBI what they saw. If they had, then why would they still be looking for his remains at some farm?

Rarely had the memory about Hoffa and Chuckie O'Brien ever popped up in family conversations anymore. It was so many years ago. But it seemed startling to me to read that the investigation was still going on over the search for Hoffa's body. I immediately called my mother to see what she remembered, and I had a few questions for her. I remembered the story as though it had just happened as well. But I was more interested in finding out how much my mother could remember about it after all this time.

I phoned Frances and started out by asking her how things were going, and what's new? I didn't want to cause her any anxiety. When I knew she was doing OK, that's when I mentioned the article and read it to her. Then I started to ask her to tell me the whole story again, whatever she could remember about that day, she and my dad were on the way to my sisters.

Frances repeated the story precisely as I had heard her tell it several times before. She didn't leave out a single detail. Pretty good for an 89-year-old and 31 years after the event.

Here's how the call went.

Refer to: "Telegraph Road Diagram"-End of Chapter 4.

"EFT" is her initials, and reply "DWT" is my initials and comments.

EFT- Well, dad (Kenneth Tubman) and I were rushing to get to Helens (daughter in Westland Twp.), and we left our house (36643 Woodward Avenue-Bloomfield Twp.) at around 2 o'clock.

Or maybe a little after, I'm not really sure the exact time. We just

wanted to get over there before John (*Helen's husband*) got home

before we went to the lake.

DWT- Which way did you go from the house?

EFT- We always thought Telegraph was the fastest way to get to Helens,

so we went down Woodward, turned right onto Maple (15 Mile

Road), and then over to Telegraph Road.

DWT-Is that when you saw the car?

EFT: Well, right after dad turned onto Telegraph, he stayed in the left

lane. It seems like it was pretty soon after we were on Telegraph

Road. I caught, out of the corner of my eye, this big burgundy or

maroon car that kind of lurched out of the driveway, right as we

were passing by the Machus Red Fox Restaurant. Then it pulled

right up behinds us, pretty close to our car.

DWT-Did you know what kind of car it was, or what color it was?

EFT-No. We found out later what kind of car it was, they said it was a

Mercury. I just knew it was some big maroon car. It was a luxury

car like a Lincoln or something like that.

DWT-Then what? (Now, she seemed to quicken her speaking pace when

she got to this part of the story).

EFT-Well, they were following behind us for a bit, and we are both in the

far-left lane. Then they started to pull up right along-side us, right next to

me, on the passenger side of the car, and they drove even with us

for a little bit.

DWT- Tell me again what was going on.

EFT-I was looking straight at the driver of the other car, and he was really

checking us out. Looking at the car, then he'd look at dad and I

again. I looked over, and I noticed that in the back seat, there was a lot of commotion going on, and I tried to figure out what was happening back there.

DWT-Like what?

EFT-There were two big men in the back seat, and they had their knees way up into their chests and were both fighting or struggling with something on the floorboards. I saw something in one of their hands that seemed like a rope or a leash. I don't know. I just remember it was like a strap or something. So, I thought maybe they're trying to keep some big old dog down on the floor in the back. But it just seemed really strange to me. So, I kept looking, and the driver kept looking back at me. Really glaring at us.

DWT-Did dad notice what was going on too?

EFT-Dad was driving, but he glanced over and saw us both staring at each other, and he said to me: "Frances-quit looking over there. That's the Mafia-quit looking." I asked him, "What do you mean, the Mafia?" I thought he was kidding around, then he said: "That's Chuckie O'Brien driving the car, turn around and stop looking at them. That's the Mafia, Frances."

DWT- How did dad know it was definitely Chuckie O'Brien?

EFT-Well I think dad knew him from the years he was at Darby's. They all came in there, and he was the one who would greet them and seat them at their tables. But he knew who the people were that came in there and sometimes the Mafia did come in to eat, it was a popular place. Till it burnt down in 1968. Dad's boss (she didn't remember, but it was Sam Boesky), may have even been involved with the Mafia. Dad wasn't, of course, but he had to know who they were so he could welcome them at Darby's. And he'd better know their names and who they are.

5-Frances Tubman/FBI Interview

DWT- So what happened in the car?

EFT-I looked at the driver again to see if he looked like he was in the Mafia and what dad was talking about, and I kind of studied him a little bit. I could only see from the top of the shoulder to the top of his head, but I noticed he had a round face and head, and he had long sideburns and a high or receding hairline. He was dressed a lot more casual than the other two men in the back seat. They had suits on, and it looked like they may have had hats on, with brims. But like I said, the driver was more casual. Then I looked back at Ken and said: "They've got a big old dog or something down on the floor, Ken. And they're trying to keep it down there." Dad said: "Who knows? Quit looking." What was strange to us was the driver was more curious about us than we were about them. We didn't feel threatened or anything, I mean they weren't doing anything to us or making us afraid of anything. We were just looking and staring at each other, except for the two men in the back seat. They weren't looking at me at all.

DWT-Then what

EFT-Then dad tried to speed up a little, and the other car drifted back in the next lane. Then it pulled up right along-side of us again, and the same thing went on. I was watching what was going on in the back seat and looking back and forth at the driver. Dad told me again to "Stop looking, it's the Mafia. Do you want to end up in the Detroit River?" He was getting upset with me for watching, but I couldn't help but look. There was definitely something going on back there. And it was strange. So, I'm looking and trying not to look at the same time.

5-Frances Tubman/FBI Interview

DWT- You told me before where the other car went after that.

EFT-Oh, yeah. So, dad slowed way down and let them go ahead of us. Then we both were watching them by now as they went up ahead in front of us. Then we saw them go across Telegraph at the turnaround up ahead of us, and they pulled over and up there behind the Raleigh House. You know, that banquet place where dad was going to go to work at one time?

DWT- Yeah. I remember him talking about that. It was only the year before all this, and he was going to take the job of running the Kosher kitchen, but someone told him it was run by the Jewish Mafia, so he turned it down. But go on, mom.

EFT-We were going really slow by then, and both dad and I were really curious about what was happening and why they were so interested in us. As we get up to about where the Raleigh House was, that was on the other side of Telegraph, and dad and I were both really looking pretty close now. And we saw the maroon car had come to a complete stop over behind the right corner of the building. It stuck out from the building about two-thirds of a car length, so we could see that it was the same car that was following us. Then as we looked off to the right, we both noticed a big garbage truck. He was just sitting there near the other car that just pulled in. Dad said it was a Detroit city garbage truck, like the one he had used over at Darby's.

DWT-So it sounds to me that dad was positive that Chuckie O'Brien was driving the maroon car next to you that day.

EFT-Well, dad knew him. I didn't know who Chuckie O'Brien was, not at that time. After we got home from visiting with Helen, you were there. A few days later, we saw his picture on the news. That's

5-Frances Tubman/FBI Interview

when I recognized him as the driver. But not at first, it was a few days later that they showed a picture of Chuckie O'Brien. But, dad's the one who knew him. He told me, "That's Chuckie O' Brien! Don't look at them!"

DWT-Tell me again, when did you and dad first realize that you most likely saw the abduction of Jimmy Hoffa that afternoon?

EFT-Well, we didn't actually 'see' Hoffa. We just saw the driver and the men in the back seat of that maroon car they say Hoffa was in.

DWT-So, you went off to Helen's-

EFT-Yes. After that, we just scratched our heads and went off to Helen's. We didn't really know what we had actually seen until it all came out in the news a couple of days later.

DWT- So did either you or dad ever tell the police or the FBI what you guys saw?

EFT-No. Dad made me promise not to repeat that to anyone. He was emphatic about that. He said, "That's the Mafia. You'll end up as minced meat." So no, I never told the police about it.

DWT-Do you think dad might have?

EFT-No. I'm positive he didn't. Your dad had that thing happen to him back at Darby's with the car that he got from his boss, and he knew not to fool around with the Mafia.

DWT- I remember that story he told us too. About the fuse that fell out of the gas tank?

EFT-Yes, do you remember that?

DWT-Yep.

The remainder of our conversation was about the news article, and we both wondered why they would still be looking for Hoffa's body somewhere. I knew what I wanted her to do, but I didn't want to get her riled up. I calmly asked her if she would be comfortable with the situation if I relayed her story to the agent named in the news article? I told her, "These guys are all probably dead, and the Mafia isn't what it used to be. Besides, I'm sure that the Hoffa family would really appreciate hearing about it" and asked if she was open to the idea.

She answered: "I guess so. Dad isn't here anymore, and I suppose it would be the right thing to do." So, I ended the call with, "Let me call you back, mom." I immediately looked up the agent in charge, who was named in the article and contacted the Detroit Field Office of the FBI. I gave him a replay of the story Frances just repeated to me moments before. He was extremely interested in hearing the story and asked me, "Would she be willing to meet with a couple of our agents at her place?" She was in an apartment in Westland near Detroit. I said, "Let me check, and I'll get back to you." At this point, I had not yet disclosed her name. Just in case she wasn't willing to talk about it with them in person.

After I spoke with mom again, I called the field office back to make the arrangements for the interview. I said My mother was OK with the idea but was a little nervous about it because it's the first time she would be telling it to the authorities. So, she asked me to mention some conditions. Like I was negotiating a deal or something. I said, "Frances needs to know the exact day and time they will be coming to see her because she always keeps her front door to the apartment locked. Let them know that she is nearly deaf and wears hearing aids. Tell them don't use the regular doorbell button. She won't be able to hear that one. There's a separate loud doorbell that she can hear, and it has a light sensor, so she sees the light go off whenever someone is at the door." Then I added, "She can't see very well, so when they get to the door, she will be able to look through the peephole to see who it is." He agreed so far. "One more thing. Tell them not to wear any hats." Mom told me that twice, "No hats." I think she had seen "The Godfather" by now and connected hats with the Mafia.

The agent agreed to all the conditions, and I called Frances to let her know they will be setting it up and getting back to us shortly. Just before the scheduled interview on June 27, 2006, I called mom again, so she was aware that the two men were safe, and she could open the door. Her neighborhood had its share of problems, so it comforted her to know in advance of any visitors. She would not open the door to a stranger ordinarily. When I phoned her, I said, "There will be two FBI agents there to see you on June 27, 2006, at (I don't recall the time), and they won't be wearing hats." She was very relieved to hear that part.

After the interview, my mother called me to tell me how it went. She described it as follows: "There were two men, and they were both very pleasant. They were here for quite some time and took a lot of notes. They asked me a lot of questions. I told them, and I made sure they knew that dad was not involved with the Mafia in any way. He just knew who they were from working at Darby's all those years. They asked me all about the maroon car, and how dad knew that it was definitely Chuckie O'Brien that was driving. I just told them what I remembered. When they left, they handed me a business card, and they told me, *"Thank you. These people aren't a threat anymore. They are all either in prison or have died. We just want to pass the story along to the Hoffa family so they can have closure."*

"That's what they said as they left the apartment and handed me their business card." She held on to their business card and put it in her 'important' drawer. I still have it in my collection of her belongings from 2007, when she moved out to live with me in Napa, California.

5-Frances Tubman/FBI Interview

FD-302 (Rev. 10-6-95)

FEDERAL BUREAU OF INVESTIGATION

Date of transcription   06/27/2006

On June 26, 2006, Elizabeth Frances Tubman Ward was interviewed at her home. After being advised of the identity of the interviewing Agents and the purpose of the interview Ward provided the following information:

Kenneth Edmund Tubman was the husband of Ward until 1987 when he died of prostate cancer. Tubman worked in the restaurant business all his life. Tubman worked for the Darby Restaurant, The Rotunda Country Inn, and the Walnut Lake Country Club. Tubman applied to work at the Raleigh House and was interviewed for a job. During the interview he was given a tour of the facility. Tubman described the cooking area to Ward as having a stainless steel kitchen, a stainless steel cutting block, a walk in freezer, a hamburger grinder, and an area to butcher their own beef. Tubman was offered a job at the Raleigh House but declined the offer after finding out the Raleigh House was owned and operated by the "mob." He knew of individuals in the "mob" because of his occupation but did not associate with them.

On July 30, 1975, Tubman and Ward were traveling to their daughters home, in Waterford, Michigan, for a family camping trip. They were driving Southbound on Telegraph Road and passed the Machus Red Fox restaurant, 6676 Telegraph Road, Bloomfield Township, Michigan. Ward described the traffic that day as being very light and that they were the only ones on the road. Soon after they passed the Machus Red Fox, at approximately 2:30 P.M., a large Maroon car, possibly an El Dorado, passed them traveling Southbound on Telegraph Road.

When the driver passed Ward and Tubman he "looked them up and down." The driver had a round face, long sideburns, red hair, a receding hairline, and was wearing a white collared shirt. Tubman recognized the driver and advised Ward that it was

b6
b7C

In the backseat of the vehicle were two white men wearing dark suits and felt hats. The two men were hunched over with their knees close to their chests. The man in the back seat on the passenger side of the vehicle had both hands down towards the floorboard. The rear passenger on the driver side had his

Investigation on   06/26/2006   at Westland, MI

File # 281A-DE-67821

SA

Date dictated

b6
b7C

by   SA

FD-302a (Rev. 10-6-95)

281A-DE-67821

Continuation of FD-302 of ___Elizabeth Francise Tubman Ward___ , On 06/26/2006 . Page ___2___

left hand down toward the floorboard and his right hand up in the air, pulling on a leash or rope. Ward could not see what was on the floorboard but speculated that they were trying to hold a dog or something down on the floor.

The Maroon vehicle passed Ward and Tubman's vehicle and proceeded South on Telegraph. The vehicle went to the Raleigh House, 25300 Telegraph Road, Southfield, Michigan, and pulled into the back. Ward recalls seeing a large garbage truck at the Raleigh house and that there was no one around the building at the time.

Ward and Tubman then continued to their daughters home and went camping. Ward and Tubman returned from camping and saw the news about James Riddle Hoffa. Ward saw pictures of _____ on the news and television and recognized him from the Maroon car. It wasn't until then that Ward and Tubman suspected that Hoffa may have been on the floorboard of the Maroon car. Tubman advised Ward never to speak of what she saw for fear of being killed.

b6
b7C

The following information was obtained through observation and interview:

Name:
Address:

Date of Birth:
Social Security
   Number:
Telephone Number:
Operators License
   Number:

Elizabeth Francise Tubman Ward
37459 Willow Lane Apt. # A17
Westland, MI
March 10, 1917

FEDERAL BUREAU OF
INVESTIGATION

Special Agent
Detroit

477 Michigan Avenue, 26th Floor
Detroit, MI 48226

Telephone: (313)
Direct Dial: (313)

REDACTED

FBI Interview-6/26/2006
Page 2 of 2

EDIT NOTE: When the unredacted version is released, the boxes will show 'Chuckie O'Brien" in place.

That's it! My mother was so relieved to have finally done what she had wanted to do for many, many years. Even when dad was alive, she had always wanted to tell the police or someone. But he insisted that she keep it to herself. I didn't ask the FBI for a transcript at the time. I didn't even realize that you could do that. We both felt good and maybe a little vindicated that the 'Tubman Family Secret' was no longer private, but safely in the right hands now. What convinced Frances she did the right thing, was the Hoffa family would have 'closure' with the information. It also was reassuring that they told her the Mafia wasn't even around anymore.

So, we thought.

A personal note about Frances.

She never wanted to get married again after Ken passed away. They had been married for forty-four years when he died in 1987 from prostate cancer. But, at around age 86, a man she and dad had known for many years, Robert Ward, had kept goading her to marry him. After all, she told me she could use the companionship, so she finally relented. The problem was that Bob's children and nobody in his family thought to inform mom before the wedding that Robert was in advanced stages of Alzheimer's. He only lived about a year after they married. That will explain why "Ward" follows her official name on the transcript. "Elizabeth Frances Tubman-Ward."

Author's Transcript Notes-

I never requested a copy of her transcript until May of 2009. It just didn't occur to me that we needed to, nor if we were allowed to ask for a copy of their notes. We both felt it was delivered into the right hands, and we left it at that. But in 2009, I ordered a copy of the transcript after speaking with Barbara Ann Crancer and learned that she had never heard the story from the FBI. It irked me that they would decide to withhold it. So, I made a request for a copy, and in a couple of months, I received the preceding document.

I do see that the agents got a couple of small details incorrectly. Either they had a couple of suggestions for Frances, and she simply agreed, or it could have just been nerves. She made a couple of mistakes on a couple of items. But the core details are still there.

For instance: It wasn't "Waterford Michigan," it was "Westland," where my sister lived at the time. It wasn't "Walnut Lake Country Club," where my dad had also worked after Darby's, it was the "Shenandoah Golf and Country Club." I worked with him there briefly as I attended Eastern Michigan for a few years. There were so many lakes around Pontiac that I would often get confused about which one was which. But I really think she had to have just been pretty nervous about the FBI sitting in front of her, and asking her lots of detailed questions.

And lastly, I never heard her call the kind of car they saw was an "El Dorado." She didn't even know car models. But in her mind, a luxury car would be something like a big 'Lincoln Continental.' Which coincidentally, looks identical to the Lincoln-

Mercury Marquis Brougham that year. She didn't know one car model from the next otherwise.

Another observation that I make from reading the official FBI transcript is that the agents had only notated that the maroon vehicle had pulled up alongside Frances and Ken just once. I am certain Frances would have told them it happened all the way down Telegraph as the two cars drove toward 10-Mile. The transcript looked more like a 'Cliff's Notes' version, instead of a full report. It was really light on the details in that respect.

I don't know who made the decision to withhold the agent's transcript from the Hoffa family. Maybe someone higher up figured it wasn't worthy of repeating. In any case, the other witness accounts mentioning "The Raleigh House" had also been filtered out, as I discovered with a call to the Hoffa family in 2009. The story never made it to them.

CHAPTER 6
The Movie "HOFFA"
2009- The Hoffa Family-Eyewitness Home-Video

2007-FRANCES TURNS 90. After my mother gave the interview in 2006, we hardly mentioned the 'Hoffa Story' again. Mom was finally able to get it off her chest by telling the FBI her story. Then in March of 2007, mom was turning 90 years old, so my brother Ken and I flew to Detroit for a surprise visit to help her and the family celebrate her birthday. We had no idea how her health really was, it was hard to determine from twenty-five hundred miles away. But we kept it a secret from mom, and when we got to Detroit, Ken and I helped arrange the party with our sister, Helen, and set up in her basement.

Looking back, it seems kind of cruel now, but at the time, we were in the 'surprise mode.' I bought twenty-five pairs of 'Schnoz glasses' from the dollar store and suggested everybody where them as a prank while we all waited in the basement for mom to come down the stairs. Then we would all yell, "Surprise!" Then we could even make a game out of it and have her try and guess who each of us were behind the 'schnoz' glasses. Since she didn't know my brother, Ken and I were going to be there-we would hold off till last and be the surprise guests. It seemed like an amusing idea.

She was pretty good at guessing some and completely stumped at guessing others. And it came down to just Ken and me who she hadn't guessed 'who's behind the glasses. Helen was bringing her around the circle to each party guest who kept their disguise glasses on till she had a chance to guess who they were. She came to my brother Ken, and she can't quite figure out who he is, so he takes off the glasses and says, "Surprise!" Mom says, "Who are you?" I ribbed my brother about that the whole trip.

But it was an eye-opener, to say the least. We realized mom's macular degeneration was getting worse. Ken and I stayed about a week then flew back home to Napa, California, where we both lived at the time. Later in the year, I kept wondering how she was doing and how she was managing everything. My sister, Helen, lived nearby, but Frances always acted independently, and Helen could only do so much for her. So, I made arrangements to fly back to Detroit again so I could get a closer look at her health situation.

I tried to set up systems and regular places for her keys, her glasses, and things she was always looking for while I was there. I saw a pile of unopened bills from credit card companies. Amazingly they were all current, but she was only able to make the interest-only payments on them. I did a budget, and she seemed to be relieved when I told her, "don't pay the credit cards anymore, mom." I put them in a rubber band and said, "you can't afford to."

I did some minor repairs for her around the apartment and got a Jitterbug phone, with huge numbers on the keypad that lit up so she could see it better. She wanted to cook me a nice dinner, so we went to Kroger's for a few things.

I wanted to see how she was able to drive, so I let her drive to the Kroger's, which was about a mile away, while I observed from the passenger seat. We got to the store, and she parked away from everybody else, then we both went in and got some things. Then she drove back to her apartment. I said, "Mom, that was amazing. I didn't know you could still see so well." She answered, "Oh, I just count the treetops, and on the sixth treetop, I turn left and go to the end of the island and turn left again into the parking lot. I park away from everyone, so I don't bump into them. Then on the way back, I count the trees again and park next to the wall in my spot."

It was that night I was talking to my wife as I sat on the kitchen floor in tears. "I don't know what to do, I really don't know what to do." MY wife Judy tried to console me, but it seemed she had the right answer and said, "Do you think your mom would consider moving in with us?" It was a hard sell. Would she ever consider leaving her daughter, Helen? And what would the family here think? It took some hard-sell tactics while I was there and later when I got home but kept trying to sell her with my best sales pitch: "Come to Napa-The Last Resort.!" I convinced her that she should try it out, and if she didn't like it, she could keep her apartment and always come back to it. That was the closing statement. She relented and decided to 'try it out.'

I made arrangements for her to come but made sure it was after she had spent that Thanksgiving in Detroit with the Kersten side of the family. Then a couple of days later, I flew back out to Detroit to help her pack and ship some things ahead. We would fly back together. While at the Detroit Metro airport, it was very crowded in the gate, and mom had to use the ladies' room. I had to keep our seats and watch our carry-on luggage, so I stayed behind as she set out for the restroom, which I could see, but it was about fifty yards away. I watched ever so curiously as she wandered towards the bathrooms. She had a cane, so she walked slowly but surely with it. I watched as she slowly drifted to the right. Instead of going straight towards the ladies' room, she disappeared behind a bank of pay-phones, and I lost her.

Then I felt a sigh of relief when she reappeared again. Now she was right in front of the entrance to the men's room. I saw a man pointing her over that way, to the other bathroom, then I watched her continue as she made her way over to the ladies' room. I thought to myself, "Good job, mom. Whew-She did it!"

Then I cautiously watched for her to resurface from the ladies' room so I could monitor her journey back to the seat where I was waiting with our bags. She started towards me but then she drifted over behind those phones again where I couldn't see her. She reappeared from behind the phone bank again and over to our seats. I was so glad that it was over. Then I noticed she was laughing and asked what was so funny. "How did it go?"

Frances admitted that she couldn't see that well and went to the wrong bathroom. She ended up in front of the men's room. "But this nice man pointed me over where the ladies' room was and got me going in the right direction." She was about to go on into the ladies' room but struck up a conversation with this other lady. Frances was talking to her for a minute or two. Then she started to notice the other lady had a cane too, just like hers. Frances looked a bit closer and began to realize it was her own reflection in a full-length wall mirror, she had been talking with. Then she turned and went into the ladies' room. She said she must have been hearing the voices from the other women nearby before she caught on. We both had a good long laugh. I told her I was going to get her a full-length mirror for her bedroom when we get back to Napa so she would have someone to talk to whenever she wanted.

Regarding Frances' health, her doctors in Detroit had two pages of medications for her. For the next several months after moving to Napa, my wife, Judy, and I became her accountability partners. Frances knocked off the miniature candy bars and knew her vitals at all times. Together we whittled it down to just two medications. One for her eyes and the other was a blood thinner for high blood pressure. She was ultimately off her diabetes medicine and all the others they had her on.

The movie 'HOFFA' with Jack Nicholson was on cable.

One night in May of 2009, Mom and I were sitting down together and decided to watch a movie and relax. I checked and saw that the film "Hoffa," with Jack Nicholson was on cable. Of course. Since neither of us had ever seen it, we watched it. We viewed it as if it were an actual documentary. In my view, it is the best of all the Hoffa movies ever made. When it came to the ending, where some young punk shoots Jimmy Hoffa as he was sitting in the back seat of a car in the parking lot of some sleazy diner, mom and I just turned and looked at each other, and we both went, "pfft! What was that?"

2009-The movie "Hoffa" had regenerated my curiosity again. Over the next several days in May of 2009, I began searching for more information. I went online and started by using the keyword: "Hoffa." I ran across so much in the way of

news articles. I found a great website with every newspaper article that contained the word 'Hoffa.' My favorite site was 'Newspapers.com.'. This was the birthing phase of my research, so I began to collect information about the Hoffa case for the very first time.

I learned early that Jimmy Hoffa had two adult children. Barbara Ann, and James Jr. Since I had four children of my own, I could relate to the sadness of the situation of their losing a father. On the other hand, I also learned about all of the violence that surrounded Hoffa's life. When I zeroed in on the aspect of Hoffa's family life, that affected me the most. It was the thought that kids and grandkids had to continue on without their father and grandfather. I have three girls and a son myself, and fathers' day was soon approaching in a few weeks. I think it motivated me to contact someone in the Hoffa family and ask if they had ever heard anything from the FBI. I knew that they surely would have been given the story by then.

I searched online for the family of Jimmy Hoffa. I saw the name James P. Hoffa, but when I discovered he was the current president of the Teamsters, I reasoned it wasn't such a good idea. I thought I'd better make the call to the other one, his daughter, 'Barbara Ann Crancer?' At least she was connected with the St Louis Attorney General's office. That would be my selection.

Barbara Ann Crancer (Hoffa's daughter)-

In the mean-time, I also ran across the name of one man who was primarily responsible for the 'taking down of the Detroit Mafia. His name was Keith Corbett. There was a phone number for him in a town near Oak Park, where I grew up, so I was familiar with the area. I tried the number, and he answered. I gave him a brief outline of the story, but the purpose of the call was to ask him if it was 'safe' to call Barbara Ann Crancer and tell her about it. He assured me it was safe, and that's when I learned about her connection to the AG office. Mr. Corbett said he was retired from law enforcement, so the story was not something of interest to him. I thanked him and ventured on to Mrs. Crancer.

I called the number I had found and spoke at first with Robert Crancer, her husband. I gave Robert an abridged version and asked his permission to talk with Barbara. He felt his wife would be very interested in hearing the story and that he would have her call me back when she was home. Later in the evening, I got the call from Mrs. Crancer and told the story in substantially more detail.

The motivation for making the call was my appreciation for the special relationship that I have with my own three daughters and son. I imagined how she must have had a special father-daughter relationship with her own dad as well. I felt she deserved to know the story in the event she had not heard it and to fill in the details if she had any questions.

It turns out that the FBI did not relay the story from my mother's interview back in 2006, as they promised they would. So, this was all brand new to her. She never heard of any eyewitness accounts connecting her father's disappearance with The Raleigh House. She didn't know that anyone had identified Chuckie O'Brien as the actual driver of the Mercury. There was no mention to her about the garbage truck that my parents saw parked and waiting behind the Raleigh House, either. Barbara Ann asked how my dad knew who Chuckie O'Brien was. I mentioned his long-term job at Darby's and the many Mafia figures who came in to eat over the years.

Then it floored me when she asked, "Why didn't your father ever say something before?" I guess I wasn't entirely expecting such a direct question. But, instantly, I recalled when dad was targeted by the Mafia back in 1968 at Darby's. The fuse in the gas tank story I mentioned earlier. It seemed the appropriate answer. It was at that point that I felt she might think I was calling apologetically about the fact he never went to the police about it in all those years. But then she went on and said: "Your dad did the right thing. The Mafia was evil and vicious back then." I hadn't really considered that I might need to seek forgiveness for my father's inaction. In her comment, "Your dad was right," I realized that she knew all too well the brutality of the Mob, in a personal way. Who was I to question why my dad did not go to the police? I guess I needed to hear that.

In closing, I asked her if the story could help her with any other leads that she already knew about. She thanked me for the story and said the information was appreciated and was quite interesting. But it doesn't appear to be "actionable." I guess that's 'legalese,' which means there was nothing she can use to go forward legally. At that point, I settled back in my chair. I said something like, "Well, if you ever do hear anything else that mentions 'The Raleigh House,' then you might consider it legitimate." She thanked me again for the call and the story.

The FBI lied to Frances-

When I hung up, I felt both relief and despair. I was relieved that I had overcome the nerve to call the Hoffa family. I was also saddened that it would not make a difference in the ongoing investigation about what happened to Hoffa after he was abducted from the Red Fox.

I was mostly upset that the FBI failed to pass the story along as they had promised my mother. It took a lot for Frances to muster up the nerve to finally go to the authorities with the information on June 27, 2006. When I told her about my call to Hoffa's daughter, she felt the FBI promise demeaned her and her willingness to come forward with it. FBI agents exploited her sincerity after they pounded her with all those questions and took notes like they were seriously interested in what she had to say to them. But the part about the Hoffa family needs 'closure' was all bullshit.

I discovered later there was some essential information that the FBI filtered from the Hoffa family. It made me question if the FBI was even serious about wanting to resolve the Hoffa case. But fortunately, that ire gave me the incentive to create the home-video interview I did with Frances, so she can tell the whole story in her own words. She was the eyewitness, so it would mean more if it came directly from her lips, and it was her image in front of the camera.

Immediately after the call with Barbara Ann, I made the video. Frances was 92 years old at the time. If I didn't get the story preserved with her direct image and testimony on camera, I might have regretted it for the rest of my life. Yes, it was kind of late in the game at 92, but she had always amazed me whenever I wasn't sure she could handle doing something, Frances had proven she was quite capable. But, of course! Frances was also a regarded member of 'The Greatest Generation.' Wasn't she?

May of 2009/The Home-Video

I set up my video camera next to the dining table and started to ask her questions on camera. I started with an easy one, "When's your birthday?" She answered my question with her own question. "June 13?" I knew in advance that she would not get the answers right on specific items if I were to ask. She would not have known who the current president was. She might not even get her own birthday correct, depending on whether she had just taken her blood pressure medication. But I wanted to demonstrate if someone were to view the video, they would know her ability to recall was waning. Although she could not remember her birthday, she remembered mine (June 13th).

I wanted her to feel relaxed, so we simply had a conversation on video. The more relaxed and comfortable she felt, the easier it would be to remember the crucial details of her story.

"Mom, do you remember the story about you and dad when you were driving on Telegraph Road back when Jimmy Hoffa disappeared?" It was a slow start, and I tried to only offer the minimum number of keywords here and there to trigger her ability to recall. At a certain point in the video interview, you will sense when it happens, she went to town and recounted the whole story in her own words.

Fortunately, this allowed me to preserve the 'Hoffa Story' being told by an actual eyewitness, in her own words, with her on video camera. At times, when she needed hand gestures to augment the story, Frances would use her hands to represent the two vehicles as they drove together down Telegraph Road. She even remembered the name of the road and vividly remembered how Telegraph road was split up the middle with a 'grassy median.' It had several lanes going in each direction. Frances then gestured with both hands representing the Mercury as it pulled behind the Raleigh House and parked 2/3 of the car length beyond the building. And she added there was the garbage truck already parked next to where the car had stopped. "A Detroit City Garbage Truck," she said, to be more specific.

She thoroughly described the driver of the Mercury once again as having a round face and long sideburns. I may have over coached her about what he was wearing. I thought that during one telling of the story years ago, she had said Chuckie O'Brien had on a white sweater. So I ended up steering her wrong on that. However, in the actual FBI transcript, Frances got it entirely right. She told the agents that O'Brien was wearing a white sport-shirt with a high collar that afternoon. In very recent research in 2019, I learned that Frances was absolutely spot on about what O'Brien wore. A white sport shirt was according to the HOFFEX memo. He was not wearing a sport-jacket or tie.

1-Ken & Frances: 1950s (The 2400 Hotel-Washington DC)

2-Ken & Frances: Mid 1970s

3-'Grandma' at Michelle's Graduation

4-2007 Took Frances to a Chicago Speakeasy-Across from Valentines Day Massacre
(L-R): Me, Helen, Frances-with Tommy-gun, Jeanne, David, Elliott Ness-(the waiter)

5-2010 Frances on the Napa River (Fish & Chips-Her Favorite)

6-2010 Last Christmas together

7-Frances' 90th Birthday ('Schnozzola' Disguises)-Ken, Helen, mom & me
   Also Used as our 'Secret Witness Protection' getup

You now have the whole story, but wouldn't it be nice to hear it directly from an eyewitness, herself?

I think most of you would agree that for Frances, at age 92, to remember something so vividly from thirty-four years earlier (as of 2009), it was nothing short of remarkable. Frances could hardly remember things like her own birthday, and she was in the very early stages of dementia. But this memorable event concerning the thirty minute-time period from 2:30 to 3:00 wound up being so deeply ingrained into her memory bank, it could not be erased. It was something she would never, ever forget.

After the call to Barbara Ann Crancer, I decided to make the following home-video. I've created a link so you can watch and hear the story directly from an eyewitness.

The Family Secret-Eyewitness Video

https://vimeo.com/jhimtg/download/431239482/c3dd73feeb
May 2009 Home-Video of Frances Tubman (Vimeo Link)
© 2020 All Rights Reserved JHIM-The Gap LLC
David W. Tubman-Author
© COPYRIGHT WARNING:
No portion of Video or other files in this link may be downloaded, copied or reproduced in any manner without the expressed written approval of the publisher and author.
All links provided are restricted only to the purchaser of this book and prohibited from being shared with anyone other than the purchaser without express written consent.
Link Issues? - Email for a new link if not able to open.
Jhimtg@gmail.com

Added One More Keyword in Online Research:

Frances passed away at age 94 on January 3, 2011, after a long-term deep cold that prompted a massive stroke. She faced being confined to a hospital bed for the remainder of her life and lost her gag reflex. Even a drop of water on her lips made her feel like she was drowning. After the call to Mrs. Crancer in 2009, I had put the Hoffa story on virtual hold. But now I began reflecting on my mother and father's life. I wasn't convinced I was to give up on learning more about the Hoffa case, and how my parent's account would fit into the overall picture.

So far, the FBI had heard it. A member of the Hoffa family has heard it. I didn't know what I was supposed to do with the eyewitness account, or was I supposed to let it die along with Frances? I went online once again. But this time, it dawned on me to add one more keyword: Not just **"Hoffa,"** I would also add the words: **"Raleigh House"** to the search bar. The news articles lit up all over the results tab. It was the first time I had ever discovered news stories about other "Raleigh House" witness accounts.

One, in particular, was October 3, 1975, in the Detroit Free Press and also in other papers around the country. In the article, it outlined that the FBI and when it went to The Raleigh House on two occasions to investigate a tip they received. The FBI called the lead, "The most reliable and workable lead they had so far." It was because of "the way in which they learned of it, which they refused to discuss." They said that "some parts of it are based on known hard facts." They would not name the witness who gave them the lead but assigned a number to them for their protection.

It turns out that the FBI and several agents went to The Raleigh House on September 22, then once again just one week later on September 29, 1975. That would have been within six weeks of the main event. The intense interest by the FBI was the first confirmation I had ever run across that would match up exactly to what my parents had always said. It had mentioned "The Raleigh House."

I thought back to my call with Barbara Ann Crancer. I wasn't about to bother her again. But it was another case of the FBI not passing information along to the Hoffa family about the Raleigh House. Barbara had never heard it mentioned before I called her either.

The two visits to the Raleigh House were so close to the disappearance, it would have been critically important information to pass along to the family. The newspapers got hold of it as it was revealed by the FBI. It is included in the FOIPA files, which I ordered on February 5, 2019, asking for the Raleigh House interview transcripts from July 30 to September 30, 1975. I received 45-pages in September 2019. The files were heavily redacted, but some information can be gleaned from them.

The Alibi

CHAPTER 7
The Alibi
The Agenda/The Fish/The Mercury

The HOFFEX Memo is a 57-page synopsis.

It contains all the accumulated evidence which was compiled by the FBI in 1976. It contains unredacted testimony and lists all of the detailed evidence the FBI had access to in 1976. I have cited it on many occasions as I was compiling this book. It is the most explicit file where much information can be found to substantiate or refute most claims by Chuckie O'Brien and others interviewed by the FBI. I urge the reader to go directly to the link in the references section: under the HOFFEX Memo. (Uploaded by The Detroit News/David Ashenfelter).

The findings in the memo bear out most of what the Tubman's have stated. But it does not, however, include some of the other critical additional details given by Ken and Frances Tubman. Reading through the HOFFEX testimony is confusing enough. Unless you study it line by line, even Columbo himself would have been confused, but at least the TV detective would always follow the facts and not just the claims.

Over the next three Chapters, I will lay out some new and substantial challenges to the O'Brien alibi. Using the Tubman account, and what they observed, I will close the door on 'The Gap,' from **2:30 to 3:30 pm** that day, and will give a brand-new factual perspective to a mystery that needs to be put to rest. It will dispel the unending mystery about what happened to Jimmy

Hoffa after he left the Machus Red Fox. There will always remain the physical remains as evidence. But simple logic will allow the reader to rest once and for all, believing you now know what eventually happened to James Riddle Hoffa. Not by forcing my opinion on you. You will be well informed to form your own conclusion.

The HOFFEX memo can be mind-boggling. But it has all the pieces, you just need to assemble them in the right order. The agents must have been wadding up the pages as they took notes and tossing them in the trash can during the two interviews with Chuckie O'Brien.

I have re-assembled them here, directly from the memo. Don't go very deep, just try to take it all at face value. I think the real truth exists amongst the lies. You simply have to sift through them with logic, because what O'Brien gave them didn't make sense at all. There are so many deceptions, one has to ask: "Why did he have to lie about the little things?" Could there be more to them than meets the eye? I think there was. But it will never be known.

Now let's dissect the alibi, but we will do it in small sections.

7A- O'Brien's Agenda: From July 29 to August 6, 1975

7B- The 16# Salmon-

7C- The 1975 Mercury Marquis Brougham-

7A- O'Brien's Agenda: From July 29 to August 6, 1975

HOFFEX Memo: (Pgs. 21-31) August 6 and August 18, 1975.

Charles Lenton 'Chuckie' O'Brien

Tuesday: July 29 - (1 day before Hoffa disappeared)

*- O'Brien said he went to dinner with the Adells.

*- Mrs. Adell said he didn't go to dinner with them.

*- O'Brien recanted. He didn't go to dinner with the Adells.

*- O'Brien said, he really went to Meadowbrook Country Club with JOE FRANCO

*- O'Brien said he was dropped off at Adells **5:00 pm.**

*- WILLIAM ROGERS Saw O'Brien at Meadowbrook between **8:00 and 10:00 pm.**

*- O'Brien calls Tony Giacalone at night, at Joey Giacalone's Apartment in St Clair Shores.

* Everything with an asterisk was either recanted or changed by O'Brien or disputed by others and then retracted by O'Brien, as related to 'The Gap' (2:30 -3:30 pm).

Wednesday: July 30 - (The day of Hoffa's disappearance)

1:00 pm- HOLMES: Chuckie O'Brien makes 2 calls from the Holmes' residence while he was there.

-Calls Tony G at SAC (TG Busy getting rubdown)/Calls Marvin Adell (left msg)

*- COB had previously given **12:30 pm** as his arrival at Holmes.

*- COB had already given **1:15-1:30 pm** as his departure from Holmes.

***2:20 pm-* Left HOLMES** for JAX (Gas/Wash)

*- O'Brien tells Vi HOLMES he was "running late for his meeting with Tony Giacalone at (SAC)."

2:15 pm- *(Changed)* Arrived at JAX (Gas first/Car wash after)

2:40 pm- *(Changed)* Left JAX Kar Wash

1:45 pm- *(Changed)* JAX alternate arrival time

2:00 pm- *(Changed)* JAX alternate departure time

2:55 pm- *(Changed)* Arrived at Southfield Athletic Club: (Didn't go to the SAC).

*- Got 2 $100 bills from Tony G. graduation gift.

The receptionist says O'Brien was not there.

*- Admitted he did not go inside SAC. O'Brien said he met with Tony G. Outside the club

*- Met Tony G. in the hallway before his haircut/After his hair-cut. Then before his hair-cut.

3:15 pm- *(Changed)* Left SAC

2:30 pm- *(Changed)* O'Brien changed his departure from SAC to 2:30 pm.

3:10 pm- *(Changed)* Arrived Joey Giacalone's work and chatted for about 10-minutes-

3:35 pm- *(Changed)* Dropped off at Trumbull at **3:35**.

- The receptionist was gone, she gets off at **4:30 pm**.

5:00 pm- JOEY VALENTI give O'Brien a ride to JAX Kar Wash in Farmington Hills

6:10 pm- Valenti and O'Brien arrive at JAX KAR WASH

6:15 pm- Adell arrives to pick O'Brien up-gets his own car washed and goes home.

7:30 pm- O'Brien said he went to dinner with the Adells

-to the Rickshaw restaurant.

- Mrs. Adell said O'Brien did not go with them to dinner.

- Called his wife, Brenda, in West Memphis, Arkansas.

* Everything with an asterisk was either recanted or changed by O'Brien or disputed by others and then retracted by O'Brien.

Author's Notes-

RE: HOLMES- One time, he arrives at **1:00** and leaves at **1:20**.
The next time it's an hour later. Using the most favorable timeline
giving O'Brien the benefit of the doubt, he still ends up with 60 to
90-minutes unaccounted for. **(2:40-4:00 pm).**

Thursday: July 31 - The day after Hoffa's disappearance

AM - COB is dropped off at Machus Red Fox.
O'Brien didn't notice that Hoffa's 1974 Green Pontiac
Grandville was parked within 100 feet from where he stood to
wait for a ride to work). Gets a lift to Trumbull.

9:30 am - COB arrives at Trumbull offices.

Noon - COB gets a message from BARBARA LIPCHICK
to call LOUIS LINTEAU regarding Hoffa not returning home
the night before.

2:00 pm - COB calls Linteau and James Hoffa Jr.

2:30 pm - COB calls Joey Giacalone for a ride, he picks up COB
and goes back to his apartment. Tony Giacalone is already
there. Tony G. got a call from Linteau about Hoffa being
missing, says there was no planned meeting the day before.
COB leaves with Joey G. to a theater, then arrives at Adells at
dinner time.

- Calls James Hoffa Jr. Borrows Adells car-goes to JPH home
"to protect them."

6:15 pm - While James P. Hoffa Jr. goes to Hoffa Lake Orion
home from his home in Troy, COB watches over James'
home and family while he's gone.

11:30 pm - JPH calls COB at Troy residence-

Wanted him to come over to the cottage right away.

Author's Notes-

-O'Brien first finds out about Jimmy Hoffa around mid-morning (Linteau left a message).

-COB Doesn't return the message regarding Hoffa being missing till after 2:00 pm.

-COB's first call to the Hoffa family (James Jr.).

-COB calls Joey Giacalone and goes to his apartment, Tony Giacalone is already there.

-COB and Joey G. went on errands, and COB was dropped off at the Adells at dinner time.

Friday: August 1 -

2:30 am - COB asks JOSEPH BANE Jr. to come to James' Troy home and goes to see James at the Hoffa residence.

4:45 am - COB leaves after James P said he knows more than he admits. James asks O'Brien to set up a meeting with Tony Giacalone. Later that morning-COB called Tony Giacalone. Sometime later in the day, COB went to Joey Giacalone's apartment.

*O'Brien's claim that evening he went to dinner (St Clair Inn) with Tony Giacalone, his wife, Zina, and Joey Giacalone, and then went home to the Adells. (Refuted)

5:55 pm - Joey Giacalone and a female (Kyle Thornton-female) left his apartment in his Cadillac.

8:45 pm - Joey returned to the apartment with unidentified guests.

***NOTE** -* Detroit Police had Joey G. under surveillance all-day long on August 1, COB was not seen in his company. COB was not seen with Tony G and Zina on August 1. Per Police notes Tony G, his wife, and Joey with a female, KYLE THORNTON. Lost in traffic. St Clair Inn, Port Huron, was 120 miles away (RT). The claim was not feasible within the time frame. When shown O'Brien's photos, employees at S.C. Inn did not see him there between **7:00 and 9:00 pm.**

Saturday: August 2 -

AM- COB calls Tony G. Haircut set up for 1:00 pm.

1:00- COB meets Tony Giacalone at SAC. (Barber confirmed)

3:30 pm- COB departs SAC goes home (Adells).

Evening- COB attends ADELLS wedding.

Sunday: August 3 - *9:00 am-*O'Brien flies back to West Memphis, Arkansas, to be with family.

Monday: August 4 - COB flies to Washington DC to meet with Fitzsimmons-passed along with a message from Tony Giacalone to stay off the news and lay low.

Wednesday: August 6 - The first FBI interview with COB at Trumbull offices. (3 hrs-30 minutes) Michigan State Police were also in attendance.

(Aug 18 int)- COB said he forgot to advise the FBI he had a meeting with Fitzsimmons in Washington DC. It was Fitzsimmons who suggested he go see the FBI in Detroit.

END OF TESTIMONY

Missed Flight to Toronto in am:

I believe there was much more to the missed Toronto flight than was given attention by FBI interviewers. He was slated to join Robert Holmes, Sr. on a union trip to Toronto on the morning of Hoffa's disappearance.

What was the real reason Chuckie O'Brien did not go to Toronto that morning? He said it was a waste of the day, and that he had to pack his belongings for the upcoming move to the south. If that was his activity for the day, then it would make perfect sense. However, the damn fish showed up, and that became the all-important mission for the day, instead of his main priority of packing up his things.

When interviewed later, Fitzsimmons stated that packing for the move was not as imminent as O'Brien made it out to be. It should not have caused him to miss the Toronto trip.

It was obviously a last-minute decision to skip the trip. Robert Holmes Sr. made a statement that he had been waiting for O'Brien at the Detroit Metro Airport in vain, as O'Brien just didn't show up. Holmes Sr. was totally unaware Chuckie wasn't going to go.

Then at **7:15 am**, O'Brien called the son, Robert Holmes Jr. for a ride from the Red Fox to Trumbull for work. Since he had to make a call to the son, Robert Holmes Jr., for a lift to work, this also shows missing the flight was a sudden decision. Otherwise, the request for a ride would not have been necessary.

The Southfield Athletic Club:

Did Chuckie O'Brien go there or not on July 30, 1975?

Which time did Chuckie lie? The first time or the times after that? O'Brien had told reporters and the FBI that at **2:20 pm** he went from Holmes to the Southfield Athletic Club to see 'Uncle Tony. While he was there, he had received two $100 bills from Tony as a graduation present for O'Brien's two children from his first marriage. He later recanted the story and said he did not go there after all, and that he lied.

There are some fascinating new details about the initial claim by O'Brien. The information is provided in the new book, "In Hoffa's Shadow," by Chuckie O'Brien's step-son, Jack Goldsmith (Pgs. 222-223). On these two pages, O'Brien attributes the false story about the club visit to Tony Giacalone. Chuckie explains that during the meeting with Tony at Joey's apartment on July 31, Uncle Tony made a request of him. He asked Chuckie to "tell anyone that asks, especially cops or journalists, that he stopped by the SAC to see him (Tony). And that he was given the $100 bills."

This was supposed to bolster the alibi about Giacalone being at the club. The rationale would follow that the alibi request from Tony would prove O'Brien's innocence. Why would Giacalone have asked O'Brien to do this for him if he knew that Chuckie would be a primary suspect and driving his son's car as well? I didn't follow the logic to that conclusion, myself. Since Tony Giacalone spent the entire day mustering up actual eyewitnesses to his being at the club all day, why would a false claim from O'Brien be needed as well? Especially if he knew

O'Brien wasn't even present. Why would he risk such a blundering request?

Other conjectures about the Southfield Athletic Club are mentioned in the HOFFEX memo.

Could it be that Chuckie O'Brien actually did go to meet with Tony after all? The agents who interrogated him said there was a witness at the SAC who said they saw O'Brien with Tony Giacalone at around **2:30 pm**. (HOFFEX, pg. 34). That sure does tie O'Brien and Tony into 'The Gap' time frame, doesn't it?

Using 'approximated times' seems to be liberally applied throughout the O'Brien testimony. FBI interviewers believe O'Brien did, in fact, go to the SAC to get last-minute instructions and possibly to bail on the plan. That conclusion is unsubstantiated with others who gave statements, however.

Joey Giacalone was spotted at the Southfield Athletic Club:

There was one other witness interviewed who worked at the SAC that day. A washing machine repairman who said he saw Tony Giacalone's son, Joey, at the SAC at **1:00** and again at about **4:00 pm** that day. If that were true, then O'Brien had no reason to drive to Lift-All and would have only had to pick up Joey from the club on Evergreen and head straight to Trumbull. Just a mention because it was included in there.

Author's Notes-

Where did Chuckie O'Brien really go?

We can rule out The Southfield Athletic Club. Not because we are convinced that he didn't go there, but because it does not alter the timeline during 'The Gap' **(2:30 to 3:30 pm).** In the Jax Kar Wash section, we will challenge whether O'Brien even had the car washed. The gas charge slip is also subject to being proven. But, because it also does not affect 'The Gap,' we shall leave it in the itinerary as well.

Hence, the only three places that Chuckie O'Brien claims he drove to that day were:

1)- **Arrived 1:15 pm** at The Holmes residence in Farmington Hills.

2)- **Arrived 2:20 pm** at Jax Kar wash (Undocumented).

3)- **Arrived 4:00 pm** at Joey Giacalone's business in Detroit. (Per Joey G.). That would only be **33.7 miles/42-minute drive-time.** Why does there always seem to be a 60 to a 90-minute 'Gap' in time? *(Because 2+2 = 4).*

"In the <u>vicinity</u> of the Red Fox at 2:30 pm"-

O'Brien admitted to driving the 1975 marron Mercury Marquis all day long. He denied that Hoffa was in the car during his travels that day. O'Brien was pressed about having been seen near The Machus Red Fox around **2:30 pm**. He admits that he did drive the Mercury somewhere 'in the vicinity' of the Machus Red Fox around that time. What destination would that have been? After scratching off the Southfield Athletic Club, all that was left was Holmes and Jax Kar Wash. Both in Farmington Hills and nowhere in the vicinity of Telegraph and 15-mile roads. Jax Kar Wash was the last stopping place, but that location is a good 12 miles away from Machus, and at least a twenty-minute drive-time.

Author's Note-

I think O'Brien just wasn't well-coached by his lone arranger Tony Giacalone. The plotters never planned on so many witnesses being involved in the main event. I read somewhere that if they had it to do over again, they would have 'popped Hoffa in the parking lot and sped off.' Instead, the story has hampered the mob's activities ever since.

To me, it appears from the start of questioning that O'Brien was left to shoot from the hip. And he wasn't one to think cleverly enough to make it up as he went along. It's like he said things as they popped into his head, whether it made sense or not.

7B- The 16# Salmon-

Such little lies to bother with, so why did he tell them? The delivery company said Carol Davis signed for a 16 lb. Coho Salmon. Other accounts say O'Brien signed for a 40 lb. Salmon. (yet another story said it was 24 lbs.). The fish company that shipped the Salmon said the fish was sealed, then sealed again, and if it leaked at all, it would be less than half a teacup. But according to O'Brien, the fish blood was leaking profusely and dripping everywhere. There was fish blood all over Chuckie O'Brien, his pants and his shirt. It was all over the front and back seats of the Mercury. When it was removed from the car, it was still dripping unceasingly, as it dripped all through the garage and onto the kitchen floor at the Holmes residence.

That was one bloody fish-It was an utter mess, it seems.

It turns out that this crucial fish delivery had become the 'sole' purpose for Chuckie O'Brien's day (sorry, that pun was intended). When it arrived at **11:45 am**-That is when Chuckie decided that he was volunteering to make the delivery to the Holmes residence, himself. This fish occupied his entire day. As soon as it arrived, he was on top of it. He had no car available because his own car was repossessed long before, and he had flown in from West Memphis, Arkansas. The primary purpose of going to Detroit was to pack up his belongings for the move.

The keys were lost for the union station wagon (disputed by others). He had to make special arrangements to borrow Joey Giacalone's brand new car to take the fish to Farmington Hills at noon. O'Brien's revised itinerary and alibi show, after the dust settles, that he had no other purpose for the extensive driving around, except to deliver the fish.

You'd have to presume that his official union business trip to Toronto was far less important than getting that Salmon over to Robert Holmes. When he said, he volunteered to deliver it. That suggests he had nothing else better to do.

7C- The 1975 Mercury Marquis Brougham-

- Why did O'Brien need to borrow THIS car?
- Did Chuckie O'Brien know Hoffa was about to be 'hit'?
- Why did Jimmy Hoffa get into this vehicle?
- Is it for sure that Hoffa was in the Mercury? (See "Jax Kar Wash" for a surprising new twist).

In the upcoming 'Jax Kar Wash' section, there is a fascinating new twist to that discussion. It may very well hold the secret to whether Hoffa was really in the car. (In answer to a recent statement floating around that he wasn't).

Who was in the Mercury, and why would Jimmy Hoffa feel comfortable about getting in?

Hoffa would put up the fight of his life, as two men would press him to the floorboard of the car. It's no consolation but, I can assure the Hoffa family that Jimmy Hoffa went down, but not without giving them the fight of his life. Hoffa's doctor said of Jimmy, "Hoffa was strong as an ox. If someone did try to kill him, he would put up a tremendous fight." Well, he did.

He knew all 3 men and believed it was reasonable they would be in the car. Obrien, although they had been estranged for months, he was still high on the loyalty list. He also knew Chuckie was an aide to Tony Giacalone, one of the two men he was to meet at **2:00.** It would also make sense that anyone else associated with Tony Provenzano would naturally be thought to be expected in the car.

There were very few people that Hoffa trusted. Although Hoffa and O'Brien were estranged, it was not a trust issue. O'Brien was still high on the list of familiarity. Hoffa even tried to contact O'Brien to make amends, but never got a return call from him. Investigations have narrowed the field to two of the following people who may have been in the car with Hoffa and O'Brien. Mafia-Wiki indicates the FBI released a memo summarizing their most reliable findings. It cited the primary suspects besides Chuckie O'Brien, was Salvatore Briguglio, his brother Gabriel, and two other brothers Stephen and Thomas Andretta. Vito 'Billy Jack' Giacalone, was also a strong suspect. Vito was with Tony Giacalone on July 26 at Hoffa's home to arrange the July 30 meeting.

The claim: "Hoffa was never in the 1975 Mercury"-

I read the recent book: "In Hoffa's Shadow" by Jack Goldsmith (Chuckie O'Brien's stepson). I ran across a claim which declares that Jimmy Hoffa was not in the Mercury driven by Chuckie O'Brien on July 30, 1975. The proof presented states that the FBI had been using the 'wrong time' all along to analyze Chuckie O'Brien's itinerary for the day. Much of that claim relies on Louis Linteaus' claim that Jimmy Hoffa made the call to him at **3:30 pm.**

Louis Linteau returned to Airport Service Lines after missing Hoffa's visit to ASL at **1:30** earlier in the day. Linteau and his close business associate, Cynthia Green, left just shortly before Hoffa stopped by. Linteau and Green had left for lunch and did a few errands.

According to Linteau, they returned to ASL at about **3:05 pm**. Then he called local 299 and spoke with Thomas Carson (Detroit Metro Airport supervisor). Then immediately after the call with Carson, he talked to Jimmy Hoffa at **3:30 pm.**

The basis of the statement "Hoffa wasn't in the Mercury" weighs almost entirely on Grand Jury testimony (September 1975) by Linteau, his close business associate Cynthia Green, his trusted driver, Elmer Reeves, and a few other paid employees.

According to the book, the grand jury testimony went like this:

-Louis Linteau said the call from Hoffa came in at **3:30 pm**.

-Cynthia Green said the call came in between **3:00 and 3:30 pm**.

-Elmer Reeves (driver) said the call came in between **3:00 and 3:30 pm**. Elmer Reeves also said he announced the call from Hoffa while Linteau was talking with Carson on the other line.

Here's why the Linteau claim is all-important for the leading statement to be true. If Hoffa called ASL at **3:30 pm**, then it would follow that Jimmy Hoffa was still alive at the **3:30** mark. If Hoffa was still alive, then he could not have been in the Mercury with O'Brien because at **4:30**, he was seen at Trumbull. That doesn't leave time for O'Brien to pick up Hoffa then drop him off somewhere else (location unknown).

I trust that I interpreted that correctly and fairly.

The sourced information draws upon a 2002 FBI report. That was 4 years before the FBI interviewed the surviving eyewitness, Frances Tubman, which didn't happen until June 27, 2006. Her eyewitness statements give brand new insight into the Hoffa case. Especially regarding the timeframe between **2:30 to 3:30 pm**. If you believe the above statement, then you probably also share the conclusion that Chuckie O'Brien did not transport Hoffa in the mercury that day.

Author's Notes-

My first question related to this statement was:

Wait a minute! Then where was Chuckie O'Brien at between the time he supposedly left Jax at **2:40 pm** until he arrived at Joey Giacalone's at **4:00 pm?** That's over an hour and a half clock time to drive those 30 miles (30-minute drive time) to Lift-All so he could return the car.

Just as it was with the initial alibi, whenever times have changed in the latter part of the testimony, you must also adjust the earlier times accordingly. It's supposed to all add up. Apparently, the aim is to create time or take it away, whichever is most convenient, and hope one hand doesn't notice that the other hand just did. Isn't that how a magician works the audience? If you add some time on the front end **(2:40** becomes **3:30),** then you take some time off the back end **(4:30** becomes **4:00),** then you create the illusion of lost time. But where does it go?

Regardless, I would recommend reading the book because it's not just about the details. It happens to be about a personal and loving relationship between a son and his father (stepfather). But when it comes to these particular details, they seem a bit skewed in Chuckie's favor over and above the factual evidence that's out there. That's even before you consider the Tubman eyewitness account. That alone refutes the statements. If truth is the desired output, then we can't let our biased emotions dictate them.

See Section 8B- LOUIS LINTEAU and his 3:30 claim regarding Jimmy Hoffa's call time.

Chapter 8
'The Gap'
Jax Kar Wash/Louis Linteau/The Raleigh House

'The Gap' is about to close in on Chuckie O'Brien because of the following sections:

8A-Jax Kar Wash-Gas? / Car Wash?

- Gas-Did Chuckie O'Brien gets gas at the time he claims?

- Wash-Did O'Brien even get the Mercury washed inside and out?

-What <u>BREAKING NEWS</u> is there? (Never mentioned before).

8B-Louis Linteau-

- Linteau claims Hoffa called him at **3:30 pm**-Is that the truth?

8C- Was Hoffa driven to The Raleigh House?

- Was the Raleigh House the final destination for Jimmy Hoffa?

- How does the Tubman's eyewitness account fit in?

- What about Central Sanitation?

8A- Jax Kar Wash/Gas

For some reason, the Jax Kar Wash was of paramount importance to O'Brien's alibi for the day. Although Jax Kar Wash was central to the alibi offered up by Chuckie O'Brien, there was no evidence to support the times he claims to have been there. On the contrary, there was overwhelming evidence to substantiate that he was NOT there that afternoon. Joseph Spitz, car wash manager, said, "No way! No way! Was either Chuckie O'Brien or the maroon Mercury at Jax Kar Wash that day?" (News article at right-Detroit Free Press August 10, 1975 Page 1 and 4).

In testimony, O'Brien gave different times for arriving and departing the Jax gas station, (Goldsmith, 2019) September. It appears to be his signature, and the receipt was dated for July 30, 1975. However, there was no time stamp on the slip. It only showed $9.26 for gas. The employee who initialed the slip was shown a photograph of O'Brien, but she said she did not see him there.

O' Brien claims he left Jax at **2:40 pm**. After figuring in the changes he made to the alibi, the only other stop would have been Lift-All on Conner Street in Detroit to return the Mercury back to Joey Giacalone.

JOSEPH SPITZ, a Hoffa case figure who died unexpectedly Thursday night.

O'Brien told the Free Press that blood from a fish he was delivering to a friend had puddled in a car he had borrowed from Joe Giacalone, son of Detroit Mafia chieftain Anthony (Tony) Giacalone.

O'Brien said he removed some blood from the car with a paper towel, then drove it to Jax Kar Wash at 31500 Grand River in Farmington, where he asked attendants to clean up the rest of the blood.

Spitz later told the Free Press: "No way, no way did anybody come out and ask us to get the blood off the seat of a car."

He also said that a search of the car wash records did not turn up O'Brien's name.

"It's just routine in police work to check everything out," said a Michigan State Police officer of the request for an autopsy, or medical examination of Spitz's body.

"There's probably nothing to it, but there's always the possibility," he said, referring to the likelihood of foul play.

"You can't tell by just a visual observation of a body."

SPITZ'S WIFE, Mary Lou, said her husband had not been threatened and said she does not suspect foul play.

Young Giacalone's car later was seized by the FBI. Laboratory tests of blood stains found in the car revealed that they were not of human origin.

Botsford General Hospital in Farmington of a ruptured duodenal ulcer and cardiac arrest.

Doctors there believe Spitz took four aspirin that morning, and that he did not know he had an ulcer.

SPITZ became a figure in the Hoffa case when he disputed C h a r l e s (Chuckie) O'Brien's a c c o u n t of his movements on the day Hoffa disappeared.

O'Brien, who describes himself as Hoffa's foster son and who has become a key figure in the Hoffa disappearance, said that he had a borrowed car "washed and gassed up" at a Farmington car wash managed by Spitz, around the time Hoffa was to keep an appointment at a suburban restaurant.

Joseph Spitz-Car Wash Manager-Denies O'Brien was there. Dies of apparent heart attack within a week. No Autopsy perfomed.

Reprint rights by Jason Milan

O'Brien said he removed blood from the car with a paper towel, then drove it to Jax Kar Wash at 31500 Grand River in Farmington.

There, O'Brien said, he showed attendants the blood on the floor and "asked them if they could clean it up for me before it dried and started to stink."

Joe Spitz, manager of the car wash, said, "No way, no way did anybody come out and ask us to get blood off the seat of a car."

O'Brien, told what Spitz had said, responded that he had a Jax Club card, which entitles cardholders to wash jobs every day for one yearly payment.

"If he'll just check his records, he'll see I was there on that Wednesday," O'Brien told the Free Press.

Spitz, contacted again, said the FBI already had checked his records for that day, and "there was no way we recorded a Mercury or anything like that."

Spitz also said a check of the car wash's records did not turn up O'Brien's name.

Two Detroit area retail fish merchants reached by the Free Press Saturday agreed that if there were any blood at all in a fish sent the way O'Brien said the salmon was sent there would not be much.

Spitz "No Way!. No Way!
FBI checked records and there was no record of the Mercury or O'Brien being there that day. Jax owner-Milen, said afterward the records came up missing. RE: O'Brien saying he used his Jax Club Card Voucher on the Mercury. Owner-Milen said "that would be impossible." The card was registered to O'Brien's own car (a Lincoln) which was not around-it had been repossessed. The voucher could not be used for any other vehicle or license number.

JAX KAR WASH Gas Receipt -No Time Stamp

BREAKING NEWS!

Joey Giacalone brought the Mercury back after Hoffa's disappearance for another thorough cleaning-*Bruce Milen*

FIRST VISIT TO JAX- Before Hoffa's disappearance.

2:20 pm- *(Approximate time).*

The time is given for getting gas and a car wash.

2:40 pm- *(Approximate time).*

O'Brien left Jax and headed for Lift-All.

Jax to Lift-All is 30.4 miles/30-minute drive time.

This would have put O'Brien arriving at Lift-All at **3:10 pm**. That's almost a full hour before Joey G. said he arrived there at **4:00 pm.** O'Brien also said after he arrived at Lift-All that he and Joey spoke for about 10-minutes before they went to Trumbull. He said before that it's only a 15-minute drive from Lift-All to Trumbull. Again, there is nearly an hour to spare.

SECOND VISIT TO JAX- After Hoffa's disappearance.

(HOFFEX, Pg. 26)

-The second visit to Jax Kar Wash gas station was at **6:10 pm** when Joe Valenti dropped him off. Joe Valenti said O'Brien called him for a ride from **4:00-4:10 pm.** Perhaps from Joey Giacalone's place.

5:00 pm- Joe Valenti and O'Brien leave Trumbull for Jax Kar Wash.

6:10 pm- Arrived at Jax.

6:15 pm- Marvin Adell picks COB up from Jax, and they go home. Adell states he got his own car gas tank filled and washed while he and Chuckie were there, Cold this be when O'Brien purchased the gas on his credit card?

7:30 pm- O'Brien went to eat with the Adells.

(Refuted/later recanted).

Author's Notes-

* RE: HOLMES-

One time he arrives at **1:00** and leaves at **1:20**.

The next time it's an hour later.

* RE: O'Brien statements-

Which visit did the gas charge slip apply- **2:30 pm or 6:10 pm?**

* RE: O'Brien suddenly changed his regular routine?

Why did O'Brien want to be dropped off at Jax, which was way over in Farmington Hills, instead of the usual drop-off at The Machus Red Fox, which was just off Maple and Telegraph? That was much closer to the Adells. Was that because Hoffa was just abducted from the Red Fox parking lot just a few hours earlier? He wouldn't want to be seen anywhere near the Red Fox.

* RE: JAX Kar Wash-

-It wasn't till September 10, 1975, his attorney (Burdick) produced a charge slip for $9.26 in gas dated July 30, 1975.

-However, there was no time stamp.

- Where is the evidence that the car wash was done?

Although the time was approximated, O'Brien stakes a large portion of his alibi on the claim about Jax Kar Wash. But the visit does not add any time to 'The Gap.'

Jax was 12 miles away from The Machus Red Fox. In light traffic, that would be a 20-minute drive.

-Was JAX the location that O'Brien said was 'in the vicinity?'

It's not clarified why the 'vicinity' wasn't pursued by the agents.

BREAKING NEWS ABOUT JAX CAR WASH

I recently contacted current Jax Car Wash co-owner, Bruce Milen, as I was asking for his review and approval of this chapter. I wanted to ask him if he could confirm or deny the information which I have presented herein regarding Jax Kar Wash. Some of it was news to him, and some things were news to me. We spoke of our dads, Ken Tubman and his father, Jack Milen, who is the founder of Jax Kar wash (1953).

I asked Bruce to describe the cleaning process if someone were to come in and say, "I've got fish blood in my car. I want you to clean it out before it starts to stink." I was referring to Chuckie O'Brien's proclaimed visit (or visits) on July 30, 1975. He enlightened me that there was a little more to that story. Joey Giacalone returned to Jax Kar Wash in Farmington Hills a few days after the disappearance of Jimmy Hoffa. Before the Mercury was impounded by the FBI on August 9.

What did Joey say? "I've got fish blood in my car. I want you to clean it out before it starts to stink." The story never got any attention. Why is this significant?

Joey Giacalone's 1975 Mercury Marquis was impounded in a pre-dawn raid on August 9, 1975. The FBI went over every fiber of the vehicle. There were three specially trained sets of scent tracing dogs that traced Hoffa's scent, which was very strong in the rear seat. Meaning he was there for sure. The small amount detected in the trunk indicated Hoffa was not placed in the trunk of the car. They also picked up a 3" long strand of Hoffa's hair (DNA tested in 2001). "Could have been there from some other time Hoffa sat in the car." That was the response by O'Brien and Joey Giacalone. Not many are aware, but they also picked up skin and blood particles that belonged to Jimmy Hoffa (Also DNA tested later in 2001).

According to Bruce Milen, it was a few days after Hoffa's disappearance that Joey Giacalone brought the Mercury back in again for another thorough cleaning because of fish blood. Look at the cleaning process once again. (Next page). There should have been very little evidence left for the FBI to be able to extract. Yet they collected a strong scent, 3" long hair, particles of blood and skin, even after two attempts to thoroughly clean the car by O'Brien and Joey Giacalone.

Jax has a very professional cleaning process, so they would have done their most complete cleaning job. Especially if someone comes in with a fishy smell problem. So, if Hoffa was ever in the car before July 30, 1975. The number of times would have been minimal since this was a brand new 1975 Mercury in mid-1975. If O'Brien had it thoroughly cleaned out at **2:20 pm** on July 30, as claimed, then there would have been little chance that hair, blood, skin, and even Hoffa's scent would still be present from a previous time in the car. There would be a fresh new canvas, so to speak. This was done BEFORE Hoffa was seen seated in the back of the Mercury an hour later. It's even more amazing there was any evidence at all after the Mercury was cleaned, vacuumed and shampooed again. This was just a few days after Hoffa had the fight of his life on July 30, and right before the Mercury was impounded. The trace evidence they collected becomes even more significant with this new information.

Now take a look at the thorough cleaning process
performed twice on the Mercury between
July 30 and August 8, 1975.

THE PROCESS: Interior-Loosen dirt using a stiff bristle
brush; Thoroughly vacuum all carpeting; Spray deodorizer
chemical; Shampoo and Rinse carpeting; Wipe down seats;
Wet/Dry vacuum again.

8B- LOUIS LINTEAU and his 3:30 claim regarding Jimmy Hoffa's call time-

According to the HOFFEX interviewer's comments, there was a lot to say about the **3:30** time given by Louis Linteau. They had several critical problems with Linteaus' claim and knew it was wrong from the start. And they had the proof to debunk it.

Linteau told the FBI that he had returned to ASL at **3:05 pm** (which is also off), and soon after, he returned made a phone call to the local #299. It was tracked down to a Mr. Thomas Carson, who was the supervisor at Detroit Metropolitan Airport. It was as he was on that call with Carson that Linteau said he received the Hoffa call. Thomas Carson remembered the call distinctly and said it was really close to **2:30 pm**. He said he distinctly heard a girl in the background announce to Linteau that "Hoffa is on the other line for you." That's when he checked his watch and ended the call with Linteau.

Linteau told the FBI that it was Elmer Reeves who told him Hoffa was on the other line and it was **3:30 pm**. Isn't that the other witness that also supported Linteau before the grand jury in September. I have heard Elmer's voice, in a Hoffa documentary, and it certainly doesn't sound 'girlish' to me at all. It pretty deep and a very masculine tone. Carson clearly said it was a female voice that said, "Hoffa is on the other line."

The other witness is a silent witness. It was the Michigan Bell Telephone Company. The FBI obtained the phone records for ASL to see when the calls were made and received on the statement. Carson's call was at **2:35 pm**, just before the next call, which was Hoffa's call in the same time frame. There were no other calls in or out besides the two during that time.

-ASL Phone records & person called:

Linteau says he returned to ASL around **3:05 pm.** However, he also states that after he returned, he made a phone call to Local 299 from ASL. (Pg. 13-HOFFEX). According to Michigan Bell Telephone records, it shows that the phone call from ASL to Local 299 was made at **2:35 pm.**

-Thomas Carson denies 3:30 call time by Linteau

THOMAS CARSON- the individual Linteau admits talking to was a Supervisor at Detroit Metropolitan Airport who said the call was really close to **2:30 pm**. Carson said that while he was speaking with Linteau, he overheard a **female** telling Linteau that "Hoffa was on the other line." Many of the other employees at ASL also failed to confirm the later time of **3:30** by Linteau. Elmer Reeves testified that he was the one who announced the call from Hoffa to Linteau.

-FBI Comments:

"Linteau's memory is bad, either genuinely or by design. Linteau also holds all his employees at ASL under his tight control, to such a degree that, as one employee has stated, "They will say anything that LINTEAU tells them to."

Jimmy Hoffa called Linteau just after he called his wife, Josephine, which was at 2:15 pm

Josephine was called first from the payphone at Dammon Hardware behind the Red Fox. She attests to it being at **2:15 pm**.

It was immediately after that he made the call to Linteau. **(2:35 pm).** Now, think about how angry and upset Jimmy Hoffa was over the no-shows to the meeting. His wife said he was hopping mad. Then he told her he was on his way home to grill the steaks as Jimmy promised her when he left the house that morning.

Given Jimmy Hoffa's anxious frustration, explain why Hoffa would then hang out in the parking lot and just relax for another 60-minutes before making his final call to Linteau at **3:30 pm?** Again, it just doesn't add up the way Linteau figures.

The following excerpts are from the HOFFEX MEMO (Pg. 13-14 January 26-27, 1976)

-Linteau claims it was 3:30 pm when the phone call came into ASL from Hoffa.

Louis Linteau was a former enemy of Hoffa before they became friends. He went to see Jimmy Hoffa on July 26, 1975. He was told all about the meeting arrangements with Tony Giacalone, Tony Provenzano, and Leonard Schultz that was set up for **2:00 pm** at the Machus Red Fox on Wednesday, July 30, 1975. He was not asked to attend the meeting at that time, but Hoffa wanted him to be there as the meeting approached the date.

The night before the July 30 meeting, Louis Linteau called Jimmy and asked what he had planned for the next day. Acting almost oblivious to the meeting that he should have been well aware of. Hoffa told Linteau, "Nothing except for the meeting at **2:00** at the Red Fox." They had spoken about it just a few days before.

ASL, at ..... p..., ...

At this point LINTEAU advises that he went into his office at ASL and made a telephone call to Local 299, IBT, Detroit, Michigan, and shortly thereafter, he was in the process to talking to an official at Detroit Metropolitan Airport, when he was advised by ELMER REEVES, an employee of ASL, that JRH was on the other line for him. LINTEAU placed the time of the HOFFA call at 3:30 p.m.

During the conversation with JRH, LINTEAU was asked by HOFFA if the GIACALONEs had called, to which LINTEAU replied in the negative. JRH then advised LINTEAU "the

LINTEAU said HOFFA called into ASL at 3:30 pm
(Pg 13 HOFFEX)

with him. He further stated to the employees that he had a meeting at the MRF with TONY G., and at this point the employee advised he could no longer hear any of the conversation. This employee has further stated that he remained inside ASL for approximately five minutes, and as he was leaving, JRH was also in the process of leaving, and they departed into the garage area together. JRH told this employee he did not have the time to discuss a problem this employee was having regarding his pension, telling the employee "I've got this meeting and I've got to meet on time".

Further investigation revealed that a telephone call was placed from ASL to Local 299, at 2:35 p.m., according to the records of the Michigan Bell Telephone Company. Further, THOMAS CARSON, Supervisor at Detroit Metropolitan Airport, the individual LINTEAU admits talking to, when the HOFFA telephone call was received at ASL, states he overheard a female tell LINTEAU that JRH was on another line. CARSON places the time of this telephone call between 1:30 and 2:30 p.m., stating that he believed it was closer to 2:30 p.m.

Numerous interviews of employees at ASL has failed to confirm LINTEAU's time of 3:30 p.m., regarding the incoming HOFFA call, nor does anyone at ASL recall answering the HOFFA call.

-14-

Phone records show call to Local #299 went out at 2:35. Carson overhears a girl in background say "Hoffa is on other line." (HOFFEX Pg 14)

On July 30 at **1:10 pm,** Linteau and his associate Cynthia Green left ASL together for some errands. They went to the bank, stopped for lunch, and Cynthia stopped at a store. They both returned to ASL right after that. He approximated the return time as **3:00 pm**. (disproven). He was told Hoffa had stopped by at **1:30.** The time doesn't align with the other events.

(HOFFEX, Pg. 17)

Author's Notes-

You can add back the misplaced one hour surrendered to the Linteau hoax. Therefore, the clock still shows 'The Gap' **2:30-3:30 pm** as still being unaccounted for by O'Brien.

<u>The LINTEAU CLAIM is FALSE: "Hoffa called me at 3:30 pm."</u>
It's an established fact that six witnesses saw Jimmy Hoffa at the Red Fox between **2:15-2:45 pm-**

In the next HOFFEX memo clip (Pgs. 19-20), you will notice the six witnesses who all saw Jimmy Hoffa at The Machus Red Fox. And five witnesses spoke with Jimmy Hoffa between **2:00 and 2:45 pm.**

What makes the witnesses who shook Hoffa's hand from **2:25-2:30** most 'reliable and certain,' was that they repeated information Hoffa mentioned that was not known by the general public. Only Jimmy Hoffa himself could have revealed that his wife, Josephine, was about to undergo cataract surgery.

The time frame for the final Hoffa sightings was from **2:30 to 2:45** at the latest. Most witnesses zeroed in on the **2:30 pm** time, however. The only problem noted by the agents was that there were no eyewitnesses to the car after it pulled out from the Red Fox driveway and turned onto Telegraph Road.

That is what makes the Tubman account extraordinarily significant. The Tubman testimony matches up precisely with all other reliable accounts about Hoffa, the Mercury, the time of day, and the other three men in the car. Even how the car veered as it hastily exited the Red Fox driveway and turned onto Telegraph Road.

The Tubmans reveal several more details that shed light on what was previously unknown to the FBI and the general public. The positive identification of the driver of the car, the car itself, the Raleigh House, the waiting Central Sanitation truck, and even a detailed description of the kitchen layout at The Raleigh House. It all leads us further down the trail to where and how he was killed. I honestly think it answers the questions concerning what happened to Hoffa's body after he was murdered.

There was also at least one eyewitness who saw Chuckie O'Brien at the Red Fox seated in the car. Of course, the Tubman's identification was not yet known. That would have made three who saw Chuckie driving the Mercury around **2:30-2:45 pm**.

their food, and paying their bills within a much more specific time frame than the witnesses themselves were able to do based on recall.

The vast majority of investigation in and around the MRF was negative regarding any sightings of JRH, or any unusual activities.

However, this investigation did reveal six eye-witnesses to the presence of JRH at the MRF on July 30, and of these witnesses, five spoke to JRH. The times of these sightings as recalled by these witnesses range from 2:00 PM to 2:45 PM. One of the witnesses, who engaged JRH in discussion, was advised by JRH that this wife, JOSEPHINE, was about to undergo a cataract operation, a fact which was not known to the general public. All of the eye-witnesses stated that JRH appeared to be waiting for someone but none could provide any information as to the method of departure JRH utilized from the MRF.

Investigation at the MRF has failed to place any other known participants to the July 30, meeting in the vicinity. However, one witness does place SALVATORE BRIGUGLIO in the MRF parking lot which is being covered under a separate section of this presentation.

CONCLUSION

Based on the extensive investigation in the vicinity of the MRF, it is felt that JRH was not physically

-19-

abducted at the restaurant on July 30, 1975. Further, it is believed that JRH arrived at the MRF at approximately 2:00 PM and departed from the area of the MRF at approximately 2:45-50 PM.

PROBLEMS

No significant problems regarding this phase of the investigation have occurred other than the lack of any eye-witnesses to JRH departure from the area of the restaurant.

INITIATED INVESTIGATION

There were 6 witnesses of Hoffa inside, at phone, in car.
Problem was the lack of eyewitnesses after car left Machus Red Fox.
(HOFFEX Pg 19-20)

Author's Notes-

Jimmy Hoffa was definitely inside the 1975 Mercury Marquis

Although the Tubmans did not see Jimmy Hoffa poking up from the flooring, the description of the two men and the commotion going on in the rear seat were telltale signs about what was happening. Their hands and body movements and the positions of their legs and knees, strongly indicates that something highly unusual was happening beneath their feet on the floor of the vehicle. Something or someone was fighting desperately to get up from the floorboards. The extreme activity indicates they were struggling against something big and powerful. It most definitely was not a 16 lb. Salmon.

What may have caused O'Brien to veer as he sped out from the driveway, may have been because Jimmy Hoffa had caught on to the idea that this was a 'hit' on him. So, he would have either tried to get out of the car or began to resist. The man from the passenger seat had to have jumped over the bench seat and into the back, to assist the other man in getting Hoffa down onto the floor. For ten minutes (5 miles), the struggle would continue as the Tubmans looked on. In the driveway of the Red Fox, there were four men, two in front and two in back.

By the time the Tubmans sighted them on Telegraph moments later, the man who was next to O'Brien in the front was now in the back, with the other man. Both were extremely busy trying to keep Hoffa down on the floor, as only two were visible above the window line of sight. (Per Tubman). The car had an opening between the two front seatbacks. That would make it easy for a man to get into the back-seat area without any difficulty.

8C- Was Hoffa driven to The Raleigh House?

The Raleigh House in Southfield was favored as the pre-eminent facility and banquet hall for hosting, because of its size, quality of food, and proximity to the freeways. They catered to many business events, weddings, bar-mitzvahs, and proms. Even my own high school prom was held there, (Oak Park High School-Class of '69). But on the darker side, The Raleigh House had been known for having direct ties to organized crime and The Purple Gang, or Jewish Mafia in Detroit. Raleigh House owner, Sammy Leiberman, was a known associate of the Mob. The Teamsters and other groups held many of their functions in one of the banquet rooms, as it was well suited for the intended purpose, the Hoffa hit.

It would be imperative to have a trusted location that was very close to The Machus Red Fox. It was conveniently close to the freeways. The Raleigh House was only 5 miles away from The Red Fox, which made for an ideal setting. It was two blocks from 696, or Northwestern Highway, which would be the route for O'Brien to quickly leave the Raleigh House and take him back to Detroit and Trumbull avenue.

The owner of the Raleigh House, Sam 'Sammy' Leiberman, was very friendly to the mob and had close affiliations with The Purple Gang of Detroit for many years. The newly remodeled kitchen was designed for the most efficient handling of meat, which had to be butchered according to Kosher tradition. This was why the Raleigh House was a favorite among the Jewish clientele in the Southfield and Oak Park area.

I'm not trying to be gruesome, but it would be well suited to dispose of a body that was murdered on the premises. The kitchen was equipped with two massive meat cutting band saws, it had all-stainless-steel tables and a central floor drain to catch the runoff. It was not a regular restaurant that was open for business all the time. It was a banquet hall and would only be open for business when it had an event scheduled. My father commented that The Raleigh House was closed as they were passing by at around **2:45-3:00 pm** on July 30, 1975.

The most ironic thing that hits me now is knowing how my father was. He was a dedicated workaholic. He most certainly would have been at the Raleigh House that day and every day, as the general manager. Perhaps he would have been the one to unlock and open the kitchen or back door to Hoffa and the men who brought him there. Instead, Ken Tubman was looking on at a short distance from across Telegraph Road, seeing this event take place. In other words, instead of being directly involved behind The Raleigh House, he was an eyewitness to it from a much safer distance.

RALEIGH HOUSE Owner and manager:

-SAM 'SAMMY' LEIBERMAN-Owner.

-Leiberman sold the restaurant on January 31, 1978, it was replaced with a multi-level office building.

-JAMES JOSEPH-General Manager at the time (July 1975).

-FBI AGENTS Investigate the Raleigh House on two dates: September 22, and September 29, 1975.

"FBI Checking Tip Hoffa Disappeared At Raleigh House."

In a newspaper article: October 3, 1975, Detroit Free Press-(Pgs. 1-A, 12-A). (Article compiled by Detroit Free Press staff writers: Jo Thomas, Ralph Orr, Remer Tyson, Billy Bowles, and Fred Girard). "The most reliable tip the FBI had so far." Although the FBI got what they called "The most reliable tip, so far," and visited the Raleigh House within weeks of the disappearance. They went there on September 22 and 29, 1975. They interviewed employees and management. They went through the dumpster that was sitting there in back-but that would have been at least three dumpster-pick-ups since August 1, the next scheduled service after July 30.

Another critical factor regarding the way the dumpster was set up is that it was only accessible from inside the restaurant. There was a trash compactor, and from there, a conveyor to the only opening of the dumpster there was. The other story about someone seeing a black Lincoln pulling up to it at mid-night of July 30, and tossing what looked like a body into it. That couldn't have happened when you already know the dumpster was NOT accessible from the exterior. It was covered and could only be fed from within the restaurant.

US Organized crime task force director Robert Ozer commented, "Information concerning the Raleigh House has come to us in a good, usable fashion. We're prepared to go forward with it to wherever it might take us." The FBI swarmed the Raleigh House as early as September 22, 1975, and returned a second time on September 29. It describes the series of dining rooms and corridors, one leading to the trash compactor. The

9-Conclusion/Author's Opinion

compactor the FBI inspected behind the building was not going to produce any evidence as it was never utilized in the murder or disposal of the body. There were at least four service pick-ups (each Friday), and bin changeouts since August 1.

There was no mention of the elaborate butcher shop and kitchen anywhere in this article. The manager of the Raleigh House was questioned, along with several of the employees. None were under suspicion. General Manager James Joseph, (The manager's job that Ken Tubman turned down in 1974) cooperated with FBI questioning. It was James Joseph who stated, "This (compactor) is fed from the inside. There is no way anybody could get at it from the outside." But the compactor would not need to be used to destroy the remains either. -I worked with my father as a storage-room clerk (Shenandoah Country Club/Bloomfield Hills, MI).

I know that the rear doors to a restaurant are always kept locked for security reasons. So, nobody can bust in and rob the restaurant. From a management perspective, it was also so an employee can't lug expensive meat or food items out the door to their car while no one is looking. Someone would have opened the rear door for the men to allow them entrance to the building and kitchen.

I also know from my work experience, that the kitchen is almost always adjacent to the rear delivery door. That provides for easy access to food deliveries and food storage during busy kitchen periods. The dumpster may be further away as it attracts flies, and that's not conducive to food preparation. It was likely located on the opposite corner of the building from the Kitchen.

The Central Sanitation Truck-

At approximately **2:45-3:00 pm**, according to what the Tubmans observed, the maroon Mercury pulled up behind the Raleigh House building (right rear corner and extended 2/3 car length beyond) the building. The Tubmans had slowed way down and were both looking in the direction of the car. Off to the right of where the vehicle had come to rest was a parked garbage truck. Ken noticed it as the same company that used to service Darby's Restaurant in Detroit when he had worked there (Tri-County or Central Sanitation).

The truck driver was sitting in the front seat, not actively doing anything except waiting, it appeared. It happened to be parked within yards of where the car was stopped. I'm sure the truck driver knew precisely where he was supposed to be parked.

The regularly scheduled dumpster pick-up for The Raleigh House was not supposed to be until two days later on Friday, August 1, 1975. It makes perfect sense that the sole purpose of the special assignment for the truck was to collect the lifeless body of Jimmy Hoffa and remove that evidence from the premises to avoid detection. Central Sanitation Services, Inc. 8215 Moran, Hamtramck, (Detroit) was incorporated the year before on June 19, 1974, by Quasarano, Peter Vitale, and Ronald Roxburgh (Son of George Roxburgh-of Local 299). Roxburgh was President, and Michael Bricker was Vice President of CS. The Central Sanitation yard also had an incinerator used to burn items. The facility was burned to the ground in March of 1976, within 8 or 9 months from Hoffa's abduction. That was just before the FBI planned to swoop down on the site and search for Hoffa's remains. When the

FBI got too close while investigating the Hoffa disappearance, the owners figured they better not take any chances.

What happened to Hoffa's Body?

Here is one expert's opinion:

James Buccellato is a Senior lecturer in criminology at Detroit's Wayne State University, author, and host of the Original Gangsters podcast. Buccellato states he "doesn't buy any of the stories that Hoffa's body was shipped back to the East Coast or even to the suburbs of Detroit. From conversations with FBI agents who worked the case, Buccellato believes the body was most likely cremated in a mob-owned incinerator just miles from the restaurant where Hoffa was last seen alive."

A profoundly accurate summation for Buccellato to make, even without having the Tubman testimony in hand.

If the FBI were more thorough in the Raleigh House lead, they would have surely interviewed all possible garbage truck drivers who worked that day and for the week afterward. To my knowledge, no drivers were ever questioned.

KEY QUESTION: Who was the driver of the Central Sanitation truck on July 30, 1975?

This was not a regularly scheduled pick-up for the driver. It was a Wednesday, and the regular day was Fridays. Since I was 24-years old in 1975, I would think a sanitation truck driver would have been about the same age or not very much older. That means the person would likely still be around to come forward about his/her unusual work-day.

It would be etched into that driver's memory bank, much the same as it was for Frances Tubman after the news broke that Hoffa was missing. The obvious connection would have become apparent as well.

FOR MORE INFORMATION-VISIT THIS LINK:

Master Resource Link-Dropbox:

https://www.dropbox.com/sh/8i7qf04e0ojy60q/AADsSmZtolI
XhswKLVOcr2FDa?dl=0

The main folder you come to contains several sub-folders.

Open the folder according to subject matter.

THE HOFFEX MEMO FOLDER:

(For a direct link to David Ashenfelter's file upload of "The HOFFEX memo", see the index section in the final pages of this book).

-THE MAIN ACTORS: (Pgs. 1-5)

-FBI Note regarding Chuckie O'Brien-central suspect: (Pg. 6)

-LINTEAU NOTES: (Pgs. 13-14)

-THE SIX WITNESSES who saw Hoffa at Red Fox:

(Pgs. 19-20)

-CHUCKIE O'BRIEN: All statements to the FBI

(Pgs. 21-31)

THE FAMILY SECRET:

FBI Transcript- Frances Tubman-Ward June 26, 2006 (2 pgs.)

FOIPA-THE RALEIGH HOUSE FILES

THE 'GAP':

NEWS ARTICLES

ADDITIONAL SOURCES

RESOURCES & RESEARCH

CHAPTER 9
CONCLUSION
Author's Opinion

You know what they say about opinions, among other things, everybody's got one. Don't take mine on as your own. Do the research and agree or disagree, that's your privilege. Everyone has that right, including me. You must remember that nobody has been charged with anything, that includes Mr. O'Brien. A court of law has never charged or convicted anyone else as well. So, everything out there and herein is considered circumstantial evidence.

A summary of The Author's Opinion -

I believe James R. Hoffa got into the maroon 1975 Mercury Marquis Brougham with three other men. The reason he got into the car was that it made sense. Obrien was now the primary aide to Tony Giacalone ('Uncle Tony'). So, it would seem perfectly natural to Hoffa that he would be the one driving the car to the actual meeting down the street. The Mercury made sense because it belonged to a Giacalone as well. The meeting being moved to another location was probably typical when an important meeting was to take place. The Raleigh House was used for many other 'official' business meetings.

Hoffa did not expect the meeting to take place inside the Red Fox, he was well aware of the dress code requiring a coat and tie for dining guests. He was dressed casually that afternoon. The other two men with O'Brien were suspect of having been one or two of the following: Sal Briguglio or his brother, Gabriel. Both brothers were closely associated with Provenzano. Or another strong candidate was 96/ 'Billy Jack' Giacalone. Vito was present at the July 26 strategy session to prepare for this meeting on July 30, and a usual attendant at meetings with Hoffa and his brother, Tony.

Hoffa and O'Brien had a rift going on since November of 1974. Some have considered that as the reason Hoffa would refuse to get into the Mercury with O'Brien. However, O'Brien remarried a month earlier, and Hoffa Jr. indicated the Hoffa was trying to smooth things over. He made several calls to O'Brien but was not able to connect. He would have been amicable by then and not hesitant to be seated behind Chuckie.

Therefore, Jimmy would have had no apprehension about O'Brien being included in the trio inside the Mercury. O'Brien, on the other hand, was establishing new relationships with Fitzsimmons and Uncle Tony, which he appreciated a bit more than Hoffa. Hoffa was holding him back, and Fitz was providing what O'Brien had been asking for and granted his wishes to relocate to Florida.

O'Brien would get a considerable bump in salary from $45k in Detroit, to $880k in his new position as union head in Florida. Everyone knew Hoffa had become a pain in the neck to the mob, and O'Brien didn't help by spreading the word that 'Hoffa was a snitch. He was going to rat out the Mafia and Fitzsimmons, and the illegal use of pension funds, making a deal with the feds, so he could run for the 1976 presidential campaign.

It could be that once Hoffa sat behind O'Brien that he began to sense something was amiss. One witness said they saw him having words with the driver, and it looked like an argument was going on. The car idled in the side drive of the Machus Red Fox briefly, as O'Brien and another man sat in the front seat, and Hoffa sat in the rear car seat with another man. The Mercury then began to pull out of the side driveway. A delivery truck driver was entering at the same time and nearly collided with the Mercury. He positively identified Jimmy Hoffa as seated in the back with three other men. He noticed a grey blanket lying on the seat between Hoffa and the other man and the shape of what looked like a shotgun (not the whole gun), underneath the grey blanket. When the FBI impounded the Mercury on August 9, they also retrieved a 12-gauge shotgun with the imprint "For Law Enforcement Only" on it.

Perhaps as the Mercury began to pull out from the Red Fox, it was at that moment that Hoffa became extremely anxious about the purpose of the ride. I would imagine he was in fight or flight mode. Hoffa may have even tried to exit the vehicle as the man sitting in front passenger seat leaped over the seatback and jumped into the rear seat compartment. He had to get into the back seat to assist the other man in subduing Jimmy Hoffa. That would explain why the car was veering as it exited and how Frances Tubman described it as it pulled out as well. That was initially caught her eye. It was the erratic driving as it had pulled out of the driveway and pulled up close behind the Tubmans.

This is where the Tubman's eyewitness account picks up on the travels of the Mercury. Their account fills in new and valuable information.

By the time O'Brien completed his right turn onto Telegraph Road and pulled up tight behind the Tubmans car, both men were in the back seat with Jimmy Hoffa pressed down onto the floor. Hoffa was not visible from this point. All three men were struggling violently in the back-seat compartment. Hoffa's doctor said he was healthy and "Strong as an ox and would fight tooth and nail to his death, should anyone try to kill him." It would be no easy task to try to contain him. Jimmy Hoffa would be pushed down by the two big men using their hands, arms, and legs. Their knees would be shoved up high into their chests while using both their hands and every ounce of strength they had to restrain Hoffa. As the photo depicts, there is a hump in the middle of the rear seat compartment, Hoffa's body must have been straddled over the hump, and his buttocks on top of it, facing up.

The man seated closest to the Tubmans, would try to work on the legs and feet, as the other man to his right, tried to contain Hoffa's arms and hands or tried to use the strap he was holding to strangle Hoffa. Frances said the man on the far right was holding a rope or strap in one hand while trying to hold something down on the floor.

When O'Brien pulled the Mercury up alongside the Tubman car and was traveling at the same rate of speed for several minutes, I wonder what he was thinking. He did that twice during the 4.9-mile journey. He drove neck and neck, and instead of looking away, as you'd expect, he was having a staring contest with Frances.

I wonder what could have been going on in his mind. Ken and Frances wondered as well. They had no clue that Hoffa was what the men were struggling with. Frances said they didn't feel threatened by it, and nothing was happening that made them feel afraid during the drive down Telegraph Road. But it was so strange. Why would the driver be so interested in them that he would glare at them? That's what caused all the curiosity in Frances and Ken Tubman.

Even though Ken had recognized who the driver was, and said "Don't look, Frances. That's Chuckie O'Brien." Frances asked, "Who's Chuckie O'Brien?" Ken replied, "That's the Mafia. Do you want to end up in the Detroit River?" She couldn't resist her curiosity and continued watching and staring.

9-Conclusion/Author's Opinion

This was the third and final time the paths of Jimmy Hoffa and Kenneth Tubman would cross.

The two vehicles were within a few feet from each other most of the distance from The Red Fox to the Raleigh House. As the Mercury sped up ahead, and Ken slowed down to create some distance, the Tubmans saw the final destination of Jimmy Hoffa. The Central Sanitation truck, which had already positioned itself adjacent to the very spot where the Mercury came to rest. Behind the right rear corner and sticking out about 2/3 car length beyond the building. The whole story about the fate of Jimmy Hoffa is told in the components of the Tubman eyewitness account, as detailed in the pages of this book and the linked video (Chapter 6).

As I have indicated earlier, it's ironic that my father would witness the final fate of Jimmy Hoffa at the Raleigh House. And instead of my father, Ken Tubman, greeting the afternoon guests at the rear door to the Raleigh House, he was witnessing it at a safe distance from across the road.

Common Q & A

Short Question & Answers-

Q: What time did the Mercury arrive at The Raleigh House?

A: 3:00 to 3:15 pm The Tubmans arrived in Westland at **4:00 pm.**
The drive-time from the Raleigh House was 45-minutes.

Q: What did O'Brien do after getting to the Raleigh House?

A: I believe his job was completed as agreed. After Hoffa was out of the
Mercury, O'Brien was sent packing.

- He went from the Raleigh House two blocks away to the 696 Freeway,
(Northwestern Hwy.), and returned the car to Joey Giacalone, and then
was dropped off at 2801 Trumbull by **4:30 pm.**

- **3:00 to 3:15 pm.** Would be when O'Brien left the Raleigh House within
minutes of his arrival.

- It also coincides entirely within the 30-40-minute drive time from The
Raleigh House to Conner street in Detroit, for an arrival time of
approximately **4:00** at Lift-All, just as Joey Giacalone prescribes.

- The other men, possibly including others perhaps already there, removed
Hoffa, still alive, and escorted him into the Kitchen area, adjacent to the
rear door. And I won't elaborate on the gruesome details about what
happened between the kitchen and the Central Sanitation truck
conveniently parked outside the kitchen door.

Q: What happened next?

A: The smaller remains were placed into the back of the Central Sanitation
truck. Without having to involve the driver, then the driver proceeded to
the Hamtramck facility for final disposition. Hoffa's remains would then
be either incinerated and/or bulldozed over. The Hamtramck facility had
burnt to the ground in March of 1976 when the FBI obtained a search
warrant and were about to exercise it.

Q: Was Hoffa murdered in the Mercury before they got to the Raleigh House?

A: No! The FBI evidence samples lifted from the Mercury indicated a murder did not take place in the car. It had to happen outside the vehicle. There would have been more blood deposited if a stabbing or shooting had occurred. Hoffa may have been partially strangled in the car.

Q: Why Central Sanitation?

A: The facility was owned by known Mafia figures. (See Chapter 8 for details).

Q: Did Chuckie know Hoffa was being hit?

A: Yes! (See Chapter 8 for details).

Q: Why would Chuckie O'Brien agree to drive the 'Hit-Car.'

A: O'Brien had money problems and was promised compensation.

Q: After seeing the counterclaims that O'Brien was innocent, do I still believe my parents?

A: Yes! Unequivocally!

You know more about Kenneth and Frances Tubman on a personal level. You know it was not a fable.

Q: Do I believe the Fish Story?

A: My one rule in life- *Never believe FISH STORIES!*

Q: Is this story actionable-or is it circumstantial?

A: Both. Even Barbara Ann Crancer told me, "There's nothing Actionable." (2009). Nobody is facing conviction over it, and never will. Whatever the FBI has, they had it long ago, and frankly-They blew it.

Q: Can someone be convicted on circumstantial evidence?

A: I'm not an attorney, but I believe they actually can.

Q: Can a Grand Jury witness lie?

A: Did Jimmy Hoffa ever lie to the Grand Jury?

Q: Are Lie Detector (Polygraph) tests reliable?
Can a pathological liar defeat one?

A: O'Brien He said he didn't want to take a polygraph exam because he "does not trust their results." But 18 years later, in 1993, he took one on the television talk show, "The Maury Povich Show." He passed and then promptly declared what he has maintained all along, that he had nothing to do with the disappearance of Jimmy Hoffa.

In the Goldsmith book, it speaks of another polygraph test, which again, he passed with flying colors.

Q: What is a lie detector test?
A: They do not actually <u>detect lies.</u>

A polygraph simply measures the physiological stimuli from the pulse and skin. That may be an indicator when a person is wired up if they are having a nervous reaction to a question. So, O'Brien was actually right not to take one in 1975. He repeated the same story for decades. He is also known to be a seasoned 'pathological liar.' So, what do we believe? Are polygraph tests reliable? Or They are not? That may have more to do with what the results show. Do we agree with them, or do we disagree?

Q: FINAL QUESTION- Aren't I just trying to pile it on a man who cannot defend himself?

A: *Absolutely, not!*

Chuckie O'Brien passed away this past February 2020. May God rest his soul. However, Charles Lenton O'Brien had 45-years to speak the complete truth. Instead, he hid behind an earthly concept called 'Omerta.' Fear is the glue that keeps that oath alive. There is nothing righteous about standing up in defense of lies. The love he had for the Hoffa family mat have been for real, but it was less important to him than his own pride in keeping it a secret.

Ultimately, truth endures forever. It does not induce fear and anxiety. Truth is reality and justice. Without it, we cannot experience inner peace. We cannot possess the happiness and joy that comes with it. If facing truth convicts us, that's because 'truth' is the conviction that follows justice. We cannot outsmart it or cover it up with lies. Truth is all-powerful and always finds its way to the surface.

That is the reason why I wrote this book.

As the FBI summarized in the Hoffa files in a report
dated Oct. 31, 1975:
the Detroit LCN family - La Cosa Nostra, or the mob.
"All sources believe that Hoffa's disappearance is directly connected
with his attempts to regain power within the Teamsters Union,
which would possibly have an effect on the LCN's control and manipulation
of Teamster Pension Funds.
The sources indicate further that even though Hoffa
cooperated with them on Teamster loans, Fitzsimmons is also cooperating
and, as such, the LCN would want to maintain conditions as they are.
It has been rumored among sources that Hoffa while attempting
to gain control of the Teamsters, may have provided information to the
Government in exchange for a favorable decision concerning the lifting of
his Union restrictions." The FBI never proved this or any other theory. But,
as the Hoffa files reveal, it was not for lack of effort.
The agency pursued virtually every tip and tidbit in its early investigation,
which yielded only a paltry amount of hard evidence,
but plenty of speculation.
Much of both centered around one man: "Chuckie O'Brien."

Tutto Fatto

Walter P. Reuther Library, Archives of Labor and Urban Affairs, Wayne State University

Young Jimmy Hoffa on a Pony
Early 1920s

FYI-James Riddle Hoffa-Trivia

DOB: Born on Valentine's Day-Feb 14, 1913
City Born: Brazil, Indiana.
Parents: John and Viola Riddle.
Ancestry: Pennsylvania Dutch/German. Viola (mother)-Irish descent.
Note: Father died 1920: Jimmy was seven years old from lung disease.
Hoffa Disappeared:
July 30, 1975 (2:30-3:00 pm)-Machus Red Fox Bloomfield Twp., MI
Hoffa Pronounced dead July 30, 1982 (Seven years later).
1995-James and Barbara Ann- (the two Hoffa Children)
Held a memorial service at Holy Trinity Church-Detroit
Hoffa Served as President-IBT (International Brotherhood of Teamsters): 1957-1971
Declared Campaign at the National Convention in Miami Beach. FL 1957
1924 The Hoffa Family Moved to Detroit-Jimmy was 11 years old
Age 17 Worked for Kroger Grocery & Baking Company
Earned 32 cents an hour/worked 4:30 am – 4:30 pm
2/3 of his pay was scrip-redeemable for food at the Kroger Company
Detroitnews.com: http://blogs.detroitnews.com/history/1999/08/27/the-day-jimmy-hoffa-didnt-come-home/
Jimmy Hoffa Net Worth at the time of death:
$13,000,000 Adjusted for inflation (celebritynetworth.com)
http://blogs.detroitnews.com/history/1999/08/27/the-day-jimmy-hoffa-didnt-come-home/
Did you also know?
Jimmy Hoffa wasn't the first union leader to be affiliated with the Mafia. . . It was already in bed:
Cornelius P. Shea founded the IBT and served as its President from 1903-1907. Shae was known to be connected w/Chicago Mafia and did some prison time for attempted murder.
Wikipedia.org: https://en.wikipedia.org/wiki/Cornelius_Shea
Jimmy Hoffa was released from prison on December 24, 1971-Christmas Eve.
It was also just 1 day before the movie "HOFFA" with Jack Nicholson was released.
Washington Post: "HOFFA" By Henry Allen/Dec 24, 1992:
Washington Post:
https://www.washingtonpost.com/archive/lifestyle/1992/12/24/hoffa/97bae349-6558-45d9-a033-4d312bcb2af9/

FYI-James Riddle Hoffa-Trivia

What is a Teamster?

A **TEAMSTER** is a truck driver or a person who drives teams of draft animals.

Further, the term often refers to a member of the International Brotherhood of Teamsters,

a labor union in the United States and Canada.

AFL American Federation of Labor 1898

CIO Congress of Industrial Organizations- 1935-1955

Separate from AFL till 1955 when both formed AFL-CIO

OCCA-Organized Crime Control Act-October 15, 1970 Under Pres. Nixon

Also: RICO-Racketeer Influenced and Corrupt Organizations Act

Wikipedia: https://en.wikipedia.org/wiki/Teamster

Appreciation

-FBI DETROIT FIELD OFFICE- (June of 2006)
Interviewed EFTubman-Ward
The FBI was the first, and we thought the only ones who needed be told
the story. The May 2006 News article about the McMasters farm dig by
the FBI startled my senses to the realization that Hoffa's body was never
found. I encouraged my mother to get it off her chest. They never
passed it on to the Hoffa family as promised.
You had your chance and missed it.

-KEITH CORBETT- (2009-Retired Detective) Phone call
I knew that Mr. Corbett would be able to tell me if it was safe to contact
Barbara Ann Crancer with the story. He assured me it would be.
Thank you, Keith.

-BARBARA ANN CRANCER- (2009-Hoffa's daughter) Phone call
I learned from Barbara that the FBI never passed the story or even the
Raleigh House portion of the story. I knew it was significant but had no
idea there was more about the Raleigh House out there when I called. I
thought mom and dad were the only ones who knew about it.
Thank you for your assurance that my father "did the right thing-
because the Mafia was ruthless."

-JAMES P. HOFFA, Jr.- (2019-Hoffa's son) Phone call
I finally got the nerve to approach James P. Hoffa, Jr. When he called,
he was genuine and made me feel at ease. I believe he appreciated
passing on the story. But like his sister, he may have also thought it
wasn't actionable. I related to his father because he and my own dad
were the same age and had that directness when they spoke, with "no
bullshit."
Thank you, Mr. Hoffa, for your sincerity.

-ERIC SHAWN- (2019 Fox News/Hoffa Documentary Series)
Phoned/Emailed
Eric was the first journalist/reporter I ran across him with the original
of three Hoffa documentaries. We spoke a few times, and I cheered him
on, even if I didn't think he was going to find Hoffa in that house in
NW Detroit. I echo Eric's encouragement for the Justice Department to
finally release the unredacted files of the Hoffa case. For answers to
questions that the Hoffa family and many people seek for a small sense
of justice.
Thanks, Eric, for taking the time to speak with me.

Appreciation

-JACK GOLDSMITH- (2019 and 2020 Author/Law Professor)
Phoned/Emailed
God bless you, Jack. I read your book as a book of hearts. To me, it was
not a crime drama. It was a book about you and your father (stepfather).
I never got to tell you how I appreciated the approach you clearly
portrayed in your personal memoirs about your life with Chuckie
O'Brien.
Thank you as well for receiving my call, despite the subject matter.

-SCOTT BURNSTEIN- (Nov 2019-Journalist/Gangster Report:
Blog) Emailed
I really encourage everyone to follow Scott on line. His was the most
informative and inspirational sites I have run across. This guy really
knows his stuff. He impressed me because he was open and not closed-
minded to something new, he hadn't heard before.
Thank you, Scott, for also reviewing the story. (1/7/2020 Gangster
Reports).

-BRUCE MILEN- (June 2020) Co-owner Jax Kar Wash
Emailed/Phoned
I appreciated the conversation we shared, Bruce. And learning that we
had mutual 'Family Secrets' surrounding the disappearance of James
Riddle Hoffa. Thank you for taking time out of your busy schedule, it
was a pleasure to meet you.

Acknowledgments

*My profound appreciation and thanks go to the following people
for their insight and support:
Thank you to my family especially my wife, Judy
for cheering me on and bringing me water and food
when I forgot all about them.
Thank you to my Mother and Father,
Kenneth E. Tubman Sr. & Elizabeth Frances Tubman
for their sacrificial love as they provided what we needed,
not always what we wanted.
Your secret is finally out, so rest in peace.
Thank you to my sister Helen, for helping to recall the events
from forty-five years ago.
Thank you to my brother, Kenneth E. Tubman, Jr.
for playing the devil's advocate in helping me weed through the details
of the story, we all knew about, and for the insight he gave.
Most of all, I thank my Lord and Savior, Jesus Christ
for giving me strength and wisdom
to suppress and overcome the stronghold of fear.
The dark force that often prevents us all from doing
what we know is right.*

DWTubman

Notes & Hyperlinks

CHAPTER 6-The Family Secret/Eyewitness Video

https://vimeo.com/jhimtg/download/431239482/c3dd73feeb
May 2009 Home-Video of Frances Tubman (Vimeo Link)
© 2020 All Rights Reserved JHIM-The Gap LLC
David W. Tubman-Author © COPYRIGHT WARNING:
No portion of Video or other files in this link may be downloaded,
copied or reproduced in any manner without the expressed written
approval of the publisher and author.
All links are restricted only to the purchaser of this book
and prohibited from being shared with anyone other than the purchaser
without express written consent.
Link Issues? - Email for a new link if this one doesn't open.
Jhimtg@gmail.com

INVESTIGATIVE AGENCIES:
-FBI: Transcript (Tubman-Ward/June 27, 2006) May 2009 Requested/Sep
2009 Received transcript.
https://www.dropbox.com/sh/fl1nb8kz7jc5pww/AACydzMDYIUGobdOO8
QAB_1da?dl=0
-FOIPA-FBI Transcripts-Raleigh House Witnesses:
Feb-2019 FOIPA Request filed: All Raleigh House-Interviews. (Over 6500 pages
to review could take months or years). Aug-2019 Revised request to only the date
between July 30, 1975, and Sep 31, 1975. Sep-2019 Received transcripts on a disc.
(Heavily redacted).
-HOFFEX MEMO:
Scribed.com-Uploaded by The Detroit Free Press (David Ashenfelter).
https://www.scribd.com/document/273002052/The-Hoffex-Memo
-O'BRIENS ALIBI: Multiple Sources
Wayne State University/Detroit Sunday Journal
https://digital.library.wayne.edu/item/wayne:DSJv2i37DSJ19970727/file
/PDF_FULL
-HOFFEX Memo: (Pgs. 21-31) Charles Lenton O'Brien August 6 and
August 18, 1975.
-LIE DETECTOR-Polygraph Testing:
https://digital.library.wayne.edu/item/wayne:DSJv2i37DSJ19970727/fil
e/PDF_FULL

Notes & Hyperlinks

NEWS AGENCIES-
THE DETROIT SUNDAY JOURNAL: "Teamsters Since Hoffa's Disappearance" July 27-Aug 2, 1997: By Michael Betzold/Journal Staff Writer "The FBI later found evidence of Hoffa's scent, hair, blood, and skin in the car's back seat."
https://digital.library.wayne.edu/item/wayne:DSJv2i37DSJ19970727/file/PDF_FULL

WASHINGTON POST:
https://www.washingtonpost.com/archive/lifestyle/1992/12/24/hoffa/97bae349-6558-45d9-a033-4d312bcb2af9/
THE DETROIT FREE PRESS:
October 3, 1975, Detroit Free Press: (Pgs. 1-A, 12-A) "FBI Checking Tip Hoffa Disappeared At Raleigh House." *(Article compiled by Detroit Free Press staff writers: Jo Thomas, Ralph Orr, Remer Tyson, Billy Bowles, and Fred Girard).*
NEW YORK TIMES/Online:
https://www.nytimes.com/1975/08/13/archives/the-hoffa-puzzle-pieces-still-dont-fit.html
NEWSPAPERS.COM:
Jax Kar Wash-Spitz denies O'Brien was there.
https://www.newspapers.com/image/622688128/
Tutto Fatto-Italian for "All Done"/Word Hippo:
https://www.wordhippo.com/what-is/the/italian-word-for-all_done.html
Blogs/Podcasts/Websites:
SCOTT BURNSTEIN-Author, blog host. "Gangster Reports" Blog by Scott Burnstein (1/7/2020) Scott Burnstein followed up with a very well written piece on a January 7, 2020 blog post called:
"The Hoffa Dumped At Raleigh House Angle Got Play by Feds In Detroit in the 2000's"
https://gangsterreport.com/the-hoffa-dumped-at-raleigh-house-angle-got-play-by-feds-in-detroit-into-2000s/
"Scott Burnstein talks Purple Gang, Jimmy Hoffa The Giacalone's" (1/29/2018)
https://www.youtube.com/watch?v=8XXd3oAqwPw
"Gangster Reports" Blog by Scott Burnstein
https://gangsterreport.com/jimmy-hoffa-made-to-disappear-at-detroit-mob-owned-central-sanitation/
ORIGINAL GANGSTERS-A True Crime Podcast
https://omny.fm/shows/original-gangsters-a-true-crime-talk-podcast/operation-motor-city-mafia-what-brought-down-the-b?in_playlist=podcast

Notes & Hyperlinks

NYTimes: https://www.nytimes.com/1975/08/13/archives/the-hoffa-puzzle-pieces-still-dont-fit.html

Biography.com: https://www.biography.com/news/jimmy-hoffa-disappearance-where-buried

James Buccellato, Ph.D. Crime Writer, and Social Scientist
https://jbuccellato.com/2015/10/15/my-book-is-coming-soon/

History; How Stuff Works: https://history.howstuffworks.com/history-vs-myth/jimmy-hoffa-body.htm
Jack Goldsmith/Author: (2019). *In Hoffa's Shadow.* New York: FARRAR, STRAUS, and GIROUX

Dan Moldea- Non-fiction author, investigative journalist.
https://www.moldea.com/

AZQuotes:
https://www.azquotes.com/quote/1086209

JHIM-Dropbox/Hyperlinks
"Jimmy Hoffa Is Missing-The Gap" by David W. Tubman

GO TO LINK- Open the following folders for related resources.

Master Resource Link-Dropbox:
https://www.dropbox.com/sh/8i7qf04e0ojy60q/AADsSmZtolIXhsw
KLVOcr2FDa?dl=0
-HOFFEX FOLDER:
-FBI Note regarding Chuckie O'Brien-central suspect: HOFFEX Pg. 6
-LINTEAU NOTES/HOFFEX Memo: Pgs. 13-14
-CHUCKIE O'BRIEN: All statements to the FBI
-SIX WITNESSES Hoffa seen at Red Fox at 2:30pm: HOFFEX Memo:
　　　Pgs. 19-20
-THE FAMILY SECRET:
-FBI Transcript- Frances Tubman-Ward June 26, 2006 (2 pgs.)
-FOIPA-THE RALEIGH HOUSE FILES
-THE 'GAP':
-NEWS ARTICLES
-ADDITIONAL SOURCES
-RESOURCES & RESEARCH

Index

PEOPLE

Adell- Marvin: O'Brien lived at the Adell house for 1-1/2 years *(54-56/111-116/130/131)*

Bane Sr.- Joseph *(48/49/115)*

Boesky- Sam: Owner-Darby's Restaurant-Detroit. Burned down July 1968. *(31-34/82)*

Briguglio- Sal, 'Sally Bugs': Suspected occupant w/Hoffa in Mercury. *(123/150)*

Buccellato, James: Senior lecturer in criminology Wayne State University Author-Host original Gangsters podcast. *(51)*

Carson- Thomas: Detroit Metropolitan Airport supervisor. *(51/124/125/135/136)*

Crancer- Barbara Ann: Hoffa's daughter. *(48/91/98/99/106/107/157/169)*

Davis- Carol: Signed for Salmon/Local 299 Union secretary *(55/121)*

FBI: *(Throughout Book)*

Franco, Joe: *(39/111)*

Giacalone- Joey: *(5/49/55-57/74/111-116/118/119/122/126/128/129/130-133/156)*

Giacalone- Tony, 'Jack': *(12/46/47/49/54/56/111/112/114-116/118/119/121/123/124/137/151)*

Giacalone- Vito, 'Billy Jack': *(34/42/45/46/124/152)*

Giacalone- Zina: *(41/115/116)*

Goldsmith- Jack: Charles L. O'Brien's stepson/Author: "In Hoffa's Shadow" Sep 2019 *(118/124/128/159/169/171)*

Green- Cynthia: ASL-Linteau, a close business associate. *(49/124/125/140)*

Reeves- Elmer: ASL driver, a former driver for Jimmy Hoffa.
(46/124/125/135/136)

Schultz- Leonard, Leo, Lenny. *(12/46/47/137)*

Spitz- Joseph: *(82/83)*

Tubman- David W.: Author of this book, son to Ken and Frances
(Throughout book)

Tubman- Frances: EFT, Frances Tubman-Ward /FBI transcript of
2006. *((Throughout)*

Tubman- Kenneth, Kenny, Ken, Jr. *(31/171/174-176))*

Tubman- Kenneth, Ken, Sr. *(Throughout)*

Valenti- Joey: Union member. Drove O'Brien to Jax on July 30, 1975, at
5:00 pm *(112/130/174)*

Vital-Peter: Central Sanitation co-owner w/Quasarano. *(46/147/173)*

Zirilli- Joseph: Detroit Mafia boss *(46/174)*

PLACES

-Local #299/O'Brien's Offices: 2801 Trumbull Ave.-Detroit, MI
(33-35/46/73-77/80/84/93/99)

-Lift-All/Joey Giacalone's work: 2679 Conner Street-Detroit, MI
(34/46/77/81/82/84/99)

-Robert Holmes Residence: 36045 Congress Court-Farmington Hills,
MI *(34/46/54-57/111/113/114/117/118/120-122/173/175)*

-Jax Kar Wash: 31500 Grand River Avenue- Farmington Hills, MI.
*(Chapter 8-All/56/57/74/75/112/120/121/123/126-
130/132/167/170/173-175/177)*

-SAC/Southfield Athletic Club: 26555 Evergreen Road-Southfield,
MI. *(12/53/74/75/112/116/118/119/175)*

-Machus Red Fox Restaurant: 6676 Telegraph Road- Bloomfield
Township, MI. (Throughout book)

-The Raleigh House: 25300 Telegraph Road-Southfield, MI.

(Throughout book)

-Meadowbrook Country Club: *(111)*

-Central Sanitation/Hamtramck (Detroit), MI:

(46/128/140/144/147/154/156/157/167/168/173-175/177)

GENERAL:

16# Alaskan Coho Salmon: *(33/34/71/78/79/92)*

1975 Mercury Marquis Brougham sedan: *(Throughout book)*

AGENDA/ITINERARY: *(27/32/71-81)*

DETROIT FREE PRESS-Metro Edition August 1, 1975 *(2/82/94)*

TIMELINES: *(27-37/73/77)*

HOFFEX Memo: *(32/36/71/72/77/84/87-91/103)*

FOIPA: Department of Justice FBI: *(68)*

The Gap- 'Gap Alert': *(1/2/7/28/31/32-36/46/66/71/72/77/82/84/88)*

La Cosa Nostra: Italian for "Our Thing" *(103)*

TEAMSTERS: *(2/5/11/13/21/62/93/103)*

TUTTO FATTO: Italian for "All Done," "That's It," "The End" *(103)*

IMAGE SCHEDULE:

-Front/Rear Covers:
Cover design by DWTubman © 2020 JHIM-The Gap LLC
-Dedication: Hoffa Family Photo-July 19, 1957
© Walter P. Reuther Library, Archives of Labor and Urban
Affairs, Wayne State University
Pg. 15: Street View of Machus Red Fox/1975 Mercury Marquis/
Remastered Bumper Sticker. design by DWTubman © 2020
JHIM-The Gap LLC
Pg. 24: (Top)-Jimmy Hoffa shooting dice w/union workers
(Bottom)-Picket Line Sep 30,1948 © Walter P. Reuther Library,
Archives of Labor and Urban Affairs, Wayne State University
Pg. 25: Three crossed paths-But Never Friends- Jimmy Hoffa and
Kenneth Tubman
design by DWTubman © 2020 JHIM-The Gap LLC
Pg. 28: 1902 Teamster Logo Teamster.org/content/teamster-history-
visual-timeline
design by DWTubman © 2020 JHIM-The Gap LLC
Pg. 38: THE SCAB Illustration by Jack London-Jan 12, 1876
Pg. 39: Joe Franco's description of Jimmy Hoffa's security technique
(Pat Zacharias-Detroitnews.com/history/1999/08/27/the-day-
jimmy-didn't-come-home/)
Pg. 52: 'Bodyguards' quotation by Jimmy Hoffa. (Original from
Playboy Magazine 1975. Reprinted in the Corpus Christi Times
on Monday, Nov 10, 1975)
Pg. 63: Google Map: (Map data © 2020 Google) Tubman Route
Wednesday, July 30, 1975
Pg. 65: GRAPHIC DIAGRAM of Telegraph Road to 10-Mile
Road. Machus Red Fox to Raleigh House from 2:30-3:00 pm
time-span.
design by DWTubman © 2020 JHIM-The Gap LLC
Pg. 66: Newspaper roll August 1, 1975, depicting headlines:
design by DWTubman © 2020 JHIM-The Gap LLC
Pg. 70: Maroon colored 1975 Mercury Marquis Brougham sedan
images design by DWTubman © 2020 JHIM-The Gap LLC
Pg. 76: Google Map: (Map data © 2020 Google)
(Top)-Chuckie O'Brien's Claimed Route (2:30-3:30)
(Bottom)-O'Brien's actual Route (Tubmans/Eyewitness)
design by DWTubman © 2020 JHIM-The Gap LLC
Pg. 77: Jimmy Hoffa's Engraved memorial plaque-Quotation
design by DWTubman © 2020 JHIM-The Gap LLC
(recreated from photograph/source unknown)
Pg. 88-89: FBI Transcript-Interview of Frances Tubman-Ward
June 26, 2006 *(2 pages)*